ECDL Module 1:
Basic Concepts of Information Technology

D0543373

Springer
London
Berlin
Heidelberg
New York
Barcelona
Hong Kong
Milan
Paris
Singapore
Tokyo

ICDL Approved Courseware
Syllabus Version 3.0

ECDL Approved Courseware
Syllabus Version 3.0

ECDL Module 1:
Basic Concepts of
Information Technology

ECDL – the European PC standard

by **John Lancaster**

Springer

BCS

The Publisher and the BCS would like to publicly acknowledge the vital support of the ECDL Foundation in validating and approving this book for the purpose of studying for the European-wide ECDL qualification.

Springer-Verlag London Ltd, Sweetapple House, Catteshall Road, Godalming, Surrey GU7 3DJ or

The British Computer Society, 1 Sanford Street, Swindon, Wiltshire SN1 1HJ

ISBN 1-85233-442-8

British Library Cataloguing in Publication Data
Lancaster, John
    ECDL module 1: basic concepts of information technology: ECDL – the European PC standard. – (European computer driving licence)
    1. Information technology
    I. Title
    004

    ISBN 1852334428

The use of registered names, trademarks etc. in this publication does not imply, even in the absence of a specific statement, that such names are exempt from the relevant laws and regulations and are therefore free for general use.

Disclaimer
Although every care has been taken by the author, the British Computer Society and the Publisher in the preparation of this publication, no warranty is given by the author, the British Computer Society and the Publisher as to the accuracy or completeness of the information contained within it and neither the author, the British Computer Society nor the Publisher shall be responsible or liable for any errors or omissions.

Printed and bound at The Cromwell Press, Trowbridge, Wiltshire, England.
34/3830-543210 Printed on acid-free paper SPIN 10792489

Preface

This book is intended to help you successfully complete the test for Module 1 of the European Computer Driving Licence (ECDL). However before we start working through the actual content of the guide you may find it useful to know a little bit more about the ECDL in general and where this particular Module fits into the overall framework.

What Is The ECDL?

The European Computer Driving Licence (ECDL) is a European-wide qualification that enables people to demonstrate their competence in computer skills. It certifies the candidate's knowledge and competence in personal computer usage at a basic level and is based upon a single agreed syllabus.

This syllabus covers a range of specific knowledge areas and skill sets, which are broken down into seven modules. Each of the modules must be passed before the ECDL certificate can be awarded, though they may be taken in any order but must be completed within a three year period.

Testing of candidates is at audited testing centres, and successful completion of the test will demonstrate the holder's basic knowledge and competence in using a personal computer and common computer applications.

The implementation of the ECDL in the UK is being managed by the British Computer Society. It is growing at a tremendous rate and is set to become the most widely recognised qualification in the field of work-related computer use.

The ECDL Modules

The seven modules which make up the ECDL certificate are described briefly below:

Module 1: Basic Concepts of Information Technology covers the physical make-up of a personal computer and some of the basic concepts of Information Technology such as data storage and memory, and the uses of information networks within computing. It also looks at the application of computer software in society and the use of IT systems in everyday situations. Some basic security and legal issues are also addressed.

Module 2: Using the Computer and Managing Files covers the basic functions of a personal computer and its operating system. In particular it looks at operating effectively within the desktop environment, managing and organising files and directories, and working with desktop icons.

Module 3: Word Processing covers the use of a word processing application on a personal computer. It looks at the basic operations associated with creating, formatting and finishing a word processing document ready for distribution. It also addresses some of the more advanced features such as creating standard tables, using pictures and images within a document, importing objects and using mail merge tools.

Module 4: Spreadsheets covers the basic concepts of spreadsheets and the ability to use a spreadsheet application on a personal computer. Included are the basic operations for developing, formatting and using a spreadsheet, together with the use of basic formulas and functions to carry out standard mathematical and logical operations. Importing objects and creating graphs and charts are also covered.

Module 5: Database covers the basic concepts of databases and the ability to use a database on a personal computer. It addresses the design and planning of a simple database, and the retrieval of information from a database through the use of query, select and sort tools.

Module 6: Presentation covers the use of presentation tools on a personal computer, in particular creating, formatting and preparing presentations. The requirement to create a variety of presentations for different audiences and situations is also addressed.

Module 7: Information and Communication is divided into two main sections, the first of which covers basic Web search tasks using a Web browser and search engine tools. The second section addresses the use of electronic mail software to send and receive messages, to attach documents, and to organise and manage message folders and directories.

This guide focuses upon Module 1.

How To Use This Guide

The purpose of this guide is to take you through all of the knowledge areas and skill sets specified in the syllabus for Module 1. The use of clear, non technical explanations and self paced exercises will provide you with an understanding of the key elements of the syllabus and give you a solid foundation for moving on to take the ECDL test relating to this Module. All exercises contained within this guide are based upon the Windows 98 operating system and Office 97 software.

Each chapter has a well defined set of objectives that relate directly to the syllabus for the ECDL Module 1. Because the guide is structured in a logical sequence you are advised to work through the chapters one at a time from the beginning. Throughout each chapter there are various review questions so that you can determine whether you have understood the principles involved correctly prior to moving on to the next step.

Conventions Used In This Guide

Throughout this guide you will come across notes alongside a number of icons. They are all designed to provide you with specific information related to the section of the book you are currently working through. The icons and the particular types of information they relate to are as follows:

information

Additional Information: Further information or explanation about a specific point.

caution!

Caution: A word of warning about the risks associated with a particular action, together with guidance, where necessary on how to avoid any pitfalls.

definition

Definition: A plain English definition of a newly introduced term or concept.

shortcut

Short Cuts: Short cuts and hints for using a particular program more effectively.

As you are working through the various exercises contained within this guide, you will be asked to carry out a variety of actions:

● Where we refer to commands or items that you are required to select from the PC screen, then we indicate these in bold, for example: Click on the **Yes** button.
● Where you are asked to key text in to the PC, then we indicate this in italics, for example: Type in the words '*Saving my work*'.

You should now be in a position to use this guide, so lets get started. Good luck

Contents

Getting Started

In this chapter you will learn how to

- *Understand the basic concepts of hardware and software and how these are related to the field of Information Technology.*

- *Understand and be able to distinguish between the different types of computer systems.*

- *Know the main parts of a personal computer system.*

1.1. Hardware/Software and Information Technology

There is a great deal of jargon used within the field of Computing and Information Technology. It is not necessary to know all of this jargon to be able to adequately function within these fields. However, knowing some jargon will help you to communicate with others concerning your use of computers. The first two terms to consider are hardware and software.

Hardware is commonly thought of as all the computer items you can touch. This is an over simplified definition, as well as a little worrying. Perhaps you should think of hardware as all the physical items of a computer system. Some of these physical items you definitely should not touch!

Software refers to the programs we run on a computer to perform certain tasks. Computer programs are as wide and varied as one's imagination performing all types of different tasks. Software also enables the various hardware devices to function together.

 Information Technology, I.T., refers to the use of this hardware and software to store and process raw facts and figures into an organised form we call information. With the right human knowledge this can be a powerful tool. Information Technology can be regarded as the use of technologies to collect, process, store and communicate information. Within the education sector the term "Information Technology" has been widened to "Information and Communication Technology", I.C.T. This has been done to recognise the growing importance of computers and similar technology in world communication.

definition

Data: The raw facts and figures.
Information: Data that is processed within context.
A number would be seen as raw data; once this has processed it may have much more meaning as perhaps a date, a part number, or an order number.

1.2. Types of Computer

Computers can broadly be grouped together according to their use and complexity. Starting with the most complex, we have:

● **Supercomputers** These are very powerful, very expensive computers that are capable of processing millions of instructions in an instant. They usually have specialist scientific or engineering functions. Examples of the uses of supercomputers are for weather forecasting, or monitoring wind flow and airframe stress of full size experimental designs in huge wind tunnels.

●

Mainframe Computers These computers usually occupy the whole of a specially air conditioned room. They would be used by large multinational organisations with great data processing needs such as banks and large insurance companies.

●

Mini Computers As technology has progressed it became possible to get the same processing power as a mainframe into a much smaller unit that would function happily without the special air-conditioned room. These scaled down mainframes are known as mini computers. Medium sized organisations would have a mini computer to cater for their considerable processing needs. They may be used to store and manage a shared database amongst many offices or to process large wage runs.

●

Personal Computers (PCs) In the late 1970s Intel Corporation managed to put the main functioning parts of a computer onto a single integrated circuit. IBM thought that there might be a need for a computer that would be small enough to fit onto a desktop. In 1981 they incorporated Intel's microprocessor into the first "Personal Computer". Many other manufacturers made clones of this computer, but the name Personal Computer stuck. Today they are simply referred to as PCs. Today's PCs have significant processing power and an immense range of uses in the workplace, at home and within schools.

Today the boundaries between many of these types of computers have become blurred as technology has progressed. It is quite difficult to draw a line between a low-end specification mainframe and a highly specified mini computer.

● **Portable Computers** This type of computer may not be any less powerful than a personal computer, but they have many different characteristics. Within this section we can place laptops, notebooks, and Personal Digital Assistants. The common characteristic is that they are all battery powered. The rechargeable battery packs can be quite heavy and early designs certainly were. Today they are considerably lighter and once charged can function for a few hours.

● **Laptops** These tend to be about the size of an A4 pad, whilst notebooks are smaller and are sometimes referred to as palmtops as they are small enough to sit in the palm of your hand. This is really the smallest type of design as they are restricted by having to be able to provide a useable keyboard. Personal Digital Assistants, PDAs, get around this problem by providing a pen, or a wand, in order to select characters. PDAs are designed to be truly hand-held whilst in use.

These types of computer are useful to provide computing power whilst on the move or at a business meeting. Any situation where mains power is not always appropriate. Such computers usually provide some method of transferring files between themselves and a larger PC.

The use of computer networks is today commonplace within many organisations. A network is a set of computers connected together so that they can communicate with and transmit data between each other. Controlling such a network would be a central computer, known as a file server or simply server, with many other computer terminals connected to it in a certain configuration. The server could possibly be a mini computer.

These computer terminals could be either intelligent or dumb terminals. A dumb terminal having no processing power, and possibly no storage capacity of its own, is entirely dependent upon the central computer. They can be no more than a unit with network connections, a screen and a keyboard. As the cost of personal computers has fallen it has become quite economical to have intelligent computer terminals that have their own processing power and storage that can operate to a certain extent independently of the central computer.

1.3. Main Parts of a Personal Computer

All computers, of whatever size, have the same basic components: input devices, the processor, output devices and auxiliary storage. Each device that goes to make up a computer system can be put into one of these categories. When trying to understand a system is helps to be able to break it down in this fashion

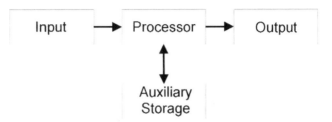

Figure 1.1 Components of a computer.

This is sometimes referred to as the 4-stage model. Auxiliary storage is sometimes called secondary storage and covers all the components used to store our data whilst we are processing it and to store this data for possible retrieval at a later time.

Figure 1.2 A common computer system.

Figure 1.2 shows the most common set-up of a personal computer system. There are more input and output devices used than the ones shown. We could use a microphone for direct voice input, a bar code reader, a scanner, or even a digital camera. Output can take the form of sound and video. We could use a plotter that draws with pens rather than prints. There are other specialist forms of input such as bank cheques that have magnetic ink on them and are read by a dedicated reader.

All the devices that attach to the processing unit are termed "peripherals." They are provided to perform a specific function. Some, such as speakers, may be provided as part of a computer package when it is purchased. Others, such as a microphone, may not.

The disk drives that store the information either cannot be seen as they are inside the base unit, or, they are accessible from the front of the base unit. Some drives are complete external devices connected to the computer with a trailing lead. The disk drives that are accessible from the front are floppy drives, CD-ROM drives, and DVD drives. The drive unseen inside the computer is the hard disk drive. An LED on the front of the base unit usually indicates when this is being accessed.

information

An LED is a Light Emitting Diode. A small coloured light often used to indicate when power is being supplied to an electrical device.

Summary

Hardware is any physical part of a computer system. Software refers to the programs that run on a computer system and allow you to do work.

There are different types of computer systems: Super computers, Mainframes, Mini's, Personal Computers and Portable Computers. Each type is basically classed according to its capability and use.

A network is a set of computers connected together and able to communicate with each other. These are under the control of a central server. The computer terminals connected to the network can be either intelligent or dumb terminals.

Computer systems consist of input devices, processors, output devices and auxiliary storage.

Peripheral devices are devices that can be attached to the processing unit to carry out a specialised job. Not all peripherals are necessarily provided as a standard part of a computer system.

Exercises

1. Briefly describe, using examples, the difference between hardware and software.

2. Name three different types of computer systems and comment on possible suitable uses for them.

3. Name three peripheral devices. State whether they are input or output devices.

4. From where does the term "PC" derive?

5. Describe the difference between a dumb terminal and an intelligent terminal.

6. Describe two advantages of using a network.

Solutions to these, and all other exercises included within this guide, can be found at the end of the guide.

Hardware

In this chapter you will learn how to

- *Understand the terms Central Processing Unit (CPU) and Microprocessor*

- *Know the functions of the CPU and how its speed is measured.*

- *Know some of the main devices for inputting data and their appropriate use.*

- *Know some of the common output devices and their use.*

2.1. Central Processing Unit

The central processing unit (CPU) lies at the heart of any computer system. It is the main component that is responsible for executing, or running, the software. The software programs are translated into a series of codes made up from 1's and 0's that the CPU can understand. A certain code will mean a certain operation needs to be carried out. A CPU has certain discrete units to help it in these tasks. For example, there is an arithmetic and logic unit (ALU) that takes care of the mathematics and logical data comparisons that need to be performed. A control register will help to make sure everything happens in the right sequence. An important task of the CPU is to access memory for the purpose of placing data there – writing data, and looking what data is stored – reading data.

It was in the late 1970's that the Intel Corporation managed to put all of these functioning parts onto a single integrated circuit that became known as a microprocessor. These much smaller devices led to the development of the personal computer. The microprocessor resides within a specially designed slot on the motherboard.

definition

Motherboard: The main circuit board inside a PC. All the other components are either slotted into or soldered onto this board.

The microprocessor communicates with the rest of the system by means of three types of buses. These buses are really no more than sets of parallel electronic conductors, sets of wires or tracks on the circuit board. The actual data travels along a data bus. The information concerning the exact location of where data is stored travels along an address bus. Signals to synchronise access to the various devices travel along the control bus.

The type of microprocessor installed within a system can greatly affect its performance. It is rare that a system would have more than one processor installed; a file server would perhaps be a good example of a system that had two processors. In the past microprocessors were given numbers rather than names. Each development was a significant improvement on its predecessor.

Originally the first IBM personal computers had an 8080 microprocessor that was quickly superseded by the 8086. Subsequently the 80286, 80386, and the 80486 have followed these. (It is common to drop the 80 and just call them 486's for example.) Today we have moved away from numbers and we have the Pentium, Pentium II and the Pentium III processors. (Intel produce Pentiums, whilst Cyrix and AMD produce 586s, which are essentially the same things!)

8080   8086   80286   80386   80486   Pentium   Pentium II   Pentium III

Improvements

Figure 2.1 The continuous improvement of microprocessors.

All microprocessors are not created equal. The later versions were all improvements upon earlier designs. These improvements invariably involved an increase in the amount of data handled at any one instance and an increase in clock speed.

The speed at which a microprocessor executes its instructions is governed by the speed of an internal clock. The number of clock pulses per second is measured in Hertz, (Hz). One pulse per second is 1 Hz. Early microprocessors ran at around 8MHz (8,000,000 pulses per second). Today Pentium II processors run at speeds up to 400 MHz and Pentium III's upto 1 GHz, (1,000,000,000 Hz). In theory a 200 MHz Pentium processor will execute instructions twice as fast as a 100 MHz Pentium processor.

caution!

There are additional factors that influence a computer's performance other than just pure clock speed.

information

The unit Hertz, Hz, was adopted in the 1930's in honour of German physicist Heinrich Hertz. Hertz completed work in the late 1880's on electromagnetic waves. He was the first person to send and receive radio waves. The term is used to indicate a measurement of the number of cycles per second.

2.2. Input Devices

The need to capture data quickly and accurately has led to the development of many different input devices each designed with a specific purpose in mind. These peripheral devices need to be able to capture the data and present it in a form that is readable by the computer system.

Some of the more common input devices are described below.

Keyboard

Keyboards are set out in a QWERTY layout, just as a typewriter, for efficient use. Although there are no standard keyboards a common layout had 102 keys. Today this has slightly increased with the inclusion of specialist keys such as those to access the Windows Start menu.

Touchpad

A touchpad is often used on a portable computer. It is a small touch-sensitive pad that replaces the mouse. By moving a finger, or small wand, over the surface the user can control the pointer. An equivalent mouse click is achieved by tapping the pad.

Joystick

Joysticks consist of a lever that can be moved in any direction to control either a pointer or, more likely, the direction of travel of a car or aeroplane within a computer game or simulation. They function in a similar fashion to a mouse, however with a mouse the pointer stops moving when the mouse stops. With a joystick, movement continues in the direction the pointer is moving. To stop the movement the lever must be returned to its upright position. Speed of movement can increase the further away from the centre the lever is positioned. Joysticks have at least two buttons, used in games to fire, change view, or to increase acceleration. Joysticks are said to give a more realistic feel to the control of some games and simulations.

Mouse

The mouse is used to control the position of the cursor on the screen and to make selections. It is possible to control the position of the cursor by using the keyboard but most users prefer to use a mouse. New users can find them a little difficult to use initially, but many soon become proficient. The cursor can change shape depending on the task being performed:

Pointer To select, e.g. menu items, files icons or graphics.

I-Beam To place the cursor into text to add or delete.

Crosshairs To draw lines, boxes, circles etc.

A single click on the left-hand mouse button will insert the I-beam cursor into text, or select an icon or graphic. A double-click on the left-hand button will open a file or select a word for editing. Clicking and holding down the left-hand mouse button whilst the mouse is moved is called "dragging". This enables items to be moved around the desktop. Clicking the right mouse button will often make visible a context sensitive short-cut menu.

Concept Keyboard

These consist of a flat bed of contact switches that are covered by a flexible membrane. A programmer can design the software to respond in a certain manner depending on which of the contacts are made. They were originally designed for young children to use enabling them, for example, to press on a symbol rather than have to try spelling a certain item. Today they are used widely in restaurants to speed up data entry and improve accuracy. They are also useful in hostile environments such as at sea where sea-salt spray may damage an ordinary keyboard.

Scanner

A scanner enables you to input graphics, photographs and text into the computer. If text is scanned it is merely a picture of the text that is captured and the text cannot be edited. OCR (Optical Character Recognition) software can be used to make the text capable of being edited as if it had been keyed in via the keyboard. Scanners are widely used by graphic intensive businesses.

Optical Mark Reader (OMR)

These readers scan a pre-printed form using infra-red light for simple marks made in specific places on the form. They are used for marking test answers and for national lottery entries. They provide a very quick method of ascertaining choices made from quite an extensive list of options.

Touch Screen

 These are specially adapted screens that let you select from the available options by the press of your finger. It is a little like selecting with a mouse. The disadvantage with such screens is that the information and options available are often limited. These are not the sort of interface to use if large amounts of information need to be portrayed or if multiple selections need to be made.

Such screens are criss-crossed by horizontal and vertical beams of infra-red light. When a finger is placed on the glass screen two of these intersecting beams are broken and the position of the finger can be detected.

These screens are very user-friendly and can be seen in such places as shopping precincts and tourist centres. They are often used in cinemas for the sale of tickets by credit card. In a shopping precinct or tourist centre they are used as a POI (Point Of Information).

Barcode Reader

Striped bar codes are now found on most products in our shops. The different thickness of the lines of the bars corresponds with different numbers. These carry information on the country of origin, manufacturer and the article itself. The reader gathers this information by measuring the bars and spaces and converting it to a machine-readable form.

Magnetic Strips

Strips of thin magnetic tape are attached to plastic cards. They are used in conjunction with a specialist reader through which the card is swiped. Playback heads similar to those in a tape recorder, read the information encoded onto the strip. These are used extensively on cash and debit cards. They are thought to have added security as they can only be read with specialist readers and dedicated software.

Magnetic Ink Character Recognition (MICR)

Bank cheques have numbers printed on them with ink that contain magnetic particles. These numbers represent the cheque number, bank sort code and the customer's account number. The banks' machines can read these characters very quickly and they are very difficult to forge. Unfortunately, until handwriting recognition is perfected, the actual amount of the cheque still has to be manually inputted.

Light Pen and Graphics Tablet

Drawing with a pen on a tablet is more natural for artists or designers who may be used to using more traditional types of tools, like pencils and brushes, than drawing by moving a mouse around. The graphics tablet can have certain libraries attached enabling an architect, for example, to select a pre-drawn graphic such as a door or light fitting. A light pen looks like a pen with a wire connecting it to the computer. These devices are mainly found in graphics studios and architects' offices.

Digital Camera

These are used just like a traditional camera. Instead of using film the images are stored in the camera's memory or directly to floppy disk. Many cameras have a small screen on which the photographs can be displayed. Unwanted pictures can be deleted directly from the camera.

Trackball

These are used just like a traditional mouse, but unlike a mouse the ball is on top and the user rolls the ball to move the cursor on the screen. These input devices are commonly used on computers where the space to use a traditional mouse is not always available.

Voice Recognition

Speech can be input into a computer system via a microphone. A spoken word is analysed and compared with those that the computer knows. If a match is found then the word is recognised. Speech recognition software enables the spoken word to be directly input into an application such as a word processing package. This has obvious advantages for speed of data input and for those with physical difficulties.

There is at present a great deal of difference in the speech recognition software at the less expensive end of the market and the highly priced packages. The less expensive have a limited vocabulary and are not very good at distinguishing between words that sound similar. These packages also require the user to speak more slowly with a pause between each word. The user needs to train the software to the sound of their voice by reading set passages and phrases thus enabling the software to work with different users. Specialist vocabularies are available for such as pathologists and accountants.

2.3. Output Devices

Output devices are peripherals that enable us to interpret the results of the computer's processing, or present these results in a form that is suitable for re-processing by computer at a later date. Without any output devices the computer becomes no more than an electronic pin-board.

Like input devices there are many output devices each designed for a particular purpose. The more common are described below, starting with the most common, the visual display unit.

Visual Display Unit (VDU)

The term "visual display unit" is used to describe any output unit that displays the result of processing in a visual form. Computer screens that use a cathode ray tube are referred to as monitors. Monitors can be colour or monochrome. Monochrome monitors can be white, orange or green on a dark background. Orange and green are supposed to be easier on one's eyes than black and white.

information

Cathode ray tubes contain an electron gun at the rear of the tube that fires electrons at phosphor dots on the back of the screen. These dots glow when the electrons hit them. The dots are very small, they cannot be seen by the naked eye. There needs to be a certain distance between the gun and the screen that increases as the size of the screen increases. This is why large screen monitors are also quite deep. This is a hindrance to the development of large screen monitors using this technology.

Resolution is a measure of the clarity of the computer display. It involves a unit known as a pixel. A pixel or 'picture element' is the smallest unit that can be displayed on a screen. A pixel on a colour monitor consists of three phosphor dots; one to display the colour red, one for the colour green and another for the colour blue. Using a mixture of these three, all other colours can be constructed. For a monitor to be able to create millions of colours it must be capable of displaying 256 different shades of each of these three colours. A typical distance between pixels is 0.28mm.

The resolution is usually expressed in terms of the number of scanned lines high by the number of pixels wide. Three standards have emerged VGA (Video Graphics Array), SVGA (Super Video Graphics Array) and XGA (Extended Video Graphics Array) which are:

VGA	640 x 480 pixels
SVGA	800 x 600 pixels
XGA	1024 x 768 pixels

Low resolution can give a jagged look to text and graphics as a result of the small number of large pixels used to form the picture. High resolution gives greater clarity and sharpness by displaying text and graphics with many smaller pixels. The difference can usually be seen on curved edges. A high resolution is therefore particularly important for design and graphic work.

Like conventional TV screens, monitors are measured diagonally from corner to corner. The standard screen has a size ratio of 4:3, width to height. Common sizes are between 14" and 19".

The quality of a monitor is also dependent upon its scan rate, referred to as the refresh rate. The scan rate is a measure of the number of times the screen is refreshed, or redrawn, per second. This is necessary as the phosphor dots that are illuminated to give the display fade rapidly. Most modern monitors can operate at different scan rates and are known as multiscan or multisync monitors. A low scan rate causes flickering and can cause eyestrain. A minimum refresh rate is said to be 75Hz.

Computer systems are set-up to display a certain number of colours on a monitor. The more colours displayed the closer to real life the images will seem. Not all systems can display all depths of colour.

LCD

LCD stands for Liquid Crystal Display. These displays rely on the fact that certain liquids alter their ability to reflect light when a voltage is applied to them. This type of display is found in digital watches and some domestic appliances. They are commonly used for laptop computers.

Printers

Printers can be categorised under two main types: Impact printers and Non-impact printers.

Impact printers have a carbon ribbon and characters are 'hammered' onto the paper through that carbon ribbon, just as with a typewriter. Non-impact printers use electrostatically charged paper to create a printed character as in the case of laser printers, or a spray of ink in the case of ink-jet or bubble printers. There can be problems with noise when impact printers are used.

Paper can be fed into a printer in a number of ways. The three main categories are:

● Friction feed, as in a typewriter, where a single sheet of paper is gripped between two rollers. Standard printing paper can be used with these printers.

● Traction Feed. Specially designed paper with holes along the edges fits over wheels with corresponding spokes for the holes, and as the wheels revolve, the paper is pulled through the printer. Continuous stationery needs to be used with these printers.

● Cut Sheet Feeder or Tray Feed. The paper is automatically drawn one sheet at a time through the printer. Standard printing paper can be used with these printers.

A dot matrix printer is an inexpensive impact printer which has lines of pins, programmed to hammer a carbon ribbon onto paper to make a dot. The characters are formed from either 9 or 24 pins. 24 pin versions produce a higher quality of print. They are quite noisy, slow, and produce medium quality text and graphics. They are very economical in use.

Daisy Wheel printers are also impact printers, but instead of using pins they have a wheel, which is supposed to resemble a daisy flower, with a different character at the tip of each petal. A tip is hammered against the paper, with carbon ribbon between them, to form a character. Different fonts are achieved by changing to a different wheel. This type of printer is very noisy and not popular.

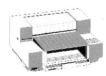

Ink-jet or Bubble printers are non-impact printers. A jet of quick drying ink is forced from a nozzle and acquires an electrical charge. The jet then passes between charged plates that deflect it to the right spot on the paper. These printers can produce cheap colour output. They are quiet but not very fast. They are best used when a relatively low, good quality output is required.

A laser printer is a fast and quiet non-impact printer. They are quite expensive but produce high quality text and graphics. Colour laser printers are particularly expensive. A toner cartridge inside the printer releases fine powder that sticks to the paper wherever it is electrically charged during the printing process. They function in a similar fashion to a photocopier.

Speakers

Speakers can be attached to a computer system in a similar way to a stereo system. They are usually small in physical size and may be built into the monitor case. Some have their own power source and amplifier. They vary in output capability but can be of a very high quality. Speakers usually require that the computer be fitted with a sound card.

definition

> **Sound Card: A hardware device in the form of a circuit board that fits into a slot on the motherboard. The purpose of the card to take care of all the sound processing for both input and output.**

Microfilm

Microfilm is used to archive documents and diagrams whilst at the same time making them available for others to view. Libraries make extensive use of microfilm, making material available to the general public without the difficulties of access and wear and tear on the originals. COM, Computer Output on Microfilm, is a technique for producing computer output directly onto microfilm.

Plotter

A plotter is used to produce large drawings created on the computer using one of the many CAD programs, (short for Computer Aided Design). Plotters have groups of pens with barrels containing ink in different colours, which are each selected in turn. On smaller plotters, up to A2 in size, the paper remains stationary and the pens move over its surface. On larger plotters the pens move simply up and down whilst the paper is rolled underneath it. These output devices are mainly found in the offices of architects or engineers.

Speech Synthesisers

This is the production of speech by electronic methods. This is achieved by a combination of software and hardware. Synthesised speech can be heard in the UK by dialling British Telecom directory enquires. When the operator has located the desired number it is delivered to the caller by a computer-generated voice.

Summary

The central processing unit (CPU) is the main component of any computer system. It is responsible for executing the software. It contains an arithmetic and logic unit (ALU) that takes care of the mathematics and logical data comparisons that need to be performed. A control register helps to make sure everything happens in the right sequence. An important task of the CPU is to access memory to place data there – writing data – and look what data is stored – reading data. All the main components of a CPU on one integrated circuit is known as a microprocessor. The clock speed of a microprocessor is measured in Hertz. One Hertz is one cycle per second.

Input devices are peripherals that are able to capture data and present it in a form that is readable by the computer system. Examples of input devices are keyboard, mouse, concept keyboard, scanner, optical mark reader, touch screen, barcode reader, magnetic strip, magnetic ink character recognition, light pen, digital camera, trackball, and voice recognition.

Output devices are peripherals that enable us to interpret the results of the computers processing, or present these results in a form that is suitable for re-processing by computer at a later date. Examples of output devices are monitors, liquid crystal displays, printers, speakers, microfilm, plotters, and speech synthesisers.

Exercises.

1. What basic functions does a microprocessor perform? How is its clock speed measured?

2. When using a mouse the shape of the cursor may change to reflect its use. Name two specific shapes of cursor and state a particular instance where it may be seen.

3. Name and briefly describe the use of three output devices other than a monitor and a printer.

4. State two factors that affect the quality of display on a computer monitor.

3

Storage

In this chapter you will learn how to

- *Know how memory capacity is measured.*

- *Understand the different types of computer memory and when they are used.*

- *Be able to compare and contrast the main types of storage devices.*

- *Know some of the factors that impact on computer performance.*

- *Understand the relationship between characters, fields, records, files and directories.*

3.1. Measuring Memory

The stated size of computer memory can be confusing at first glance. Why is a Kilo 1024 and not 1000? A little time spent studying the origins, design and development of computer systems can help to unravel this mystery.

Computers are essentially digital devices. They work with data that is physically at one of two different voltage levels. In practice these two levels are referred to as '0' and '1'. For our purposes it does not really matter if the levels are 0V and +5V, which are typical values, just that there are two different entities. The computer needs to detect a certain level that is some distance from the other. This is sometimes likened to the brain receiving pulses of energy via our nervous system.

As we use just these two levels, binary arithmetic has been adopted to help when working at this machine level. A '0' to represent one level, or perhaps false, and '1' to represent the opposite level, or perhaps true.

A single binary digit, a 1 or a 0, is called a Bit. E.g. 1.
Eight bits are a Byte. E.g. 10011101
Four bits, half a byte, are called a Nibble. E.g. 1001.

8 bits, or a byte, are important as some of the first basic microprocessors could only work with data 8 bits long. They were said to have a word length of 8 bits. It is from this premise that further design work was based and has since developed.

Each memory location is capable of holding a byte of data, 8 bits, and must be given a discrete address. Just the same way as each phone number needs to be individual. As with phone numbers we need to add more digits if we want to have more capacity for individual numbers. Consider just having 2 binary digits to address all the memory locations. We could in fact only have four different addresses:

0 0
0 1
1 0
1 1

If we add just one more digit, or bit, we could have eight different addresses:

0 0 0
0 0 1
0 1 0
0 1 1
1 0 0
1 0 1
1 1 0
1 1 1

We could go on like this adding another bit again and again and working out the capacity, but it is actually much easier to do this mathematically. The binary number system is termed base 2, 2 digits 1 and 0. If we use this base number and multiply it by the power of the number of bits, it will give us the number of discrete locations possible. For example $2^2 = 4$, $2^3 = 8$, and $2^4 = 16$:

0 0 0 0   1 0 0 0
0 0 0 1   1 0 0 1
0 0 1 0   1 0 1 0
0 0 1 1   1 0 1 1
0 1 0 0   1 1 0 0
0 1 0 1   1 1 0 1
0 1 1 0   1 1 1 0
0 1 1 1   1 1 1 1

16 different memory locations would not be much use. As we have already stated early microprocessors could handle 8 bits all at once. This would give us $2^8 = 256$ different locations. Memory chips are made up then of units of 256 different locations.

This is still not really enough. If we added another line to our address bus to access these locations we could use this to 'switch on' two different sets of 256. If this line was a 0 we could be addressing the first 256 locations and if it was a 1 we could be addressing the second 256 locations. Now we could have memory that was 512 locations big. It follows then that if we had two extra lines we could have 4 x 256 = 1024 different locations. This 1024 became known in computing terms as a Kilobyte of memory.

If in computing a Kilobyte, Kb is actually 1024 bytes then:

● A Megabyte, Mb is actually 1024 x 1024 bytes = 1,048,576 bytes.
● A Gigabyte is 1024 x 1,048,576 = 1,073,741,824 bytes.

It doesn't really matter if you cannot remember the exact values. If it is easier, think of them with their correct values of Kilo = 1000; Mega = 1,000,000; and Giga = 1,000,000,000.

Now let's get an idea of how all this relates to your work. It takes one byte to hold the binary code for each letter on the keyboard, for example 01100101 is 'A' and 10010111 is 'a'. Each character is represented by a byte of data. A word will contain lots of bytes, one for each character. A sentence further increases the bytes used, don't forget the spaces and punctuation marks. Information containing the layout and fonts used also needs to be stored. A whole document saved as a file on a floppy disk can take up kilobytes of space.

A field of information may be of a certain format, consisting of a number of characters. A whole number may actually take 2 bytes of storage. A complete set of fields related to a single entity, for example a person, form a complete record. This record then can be many bytes. If we have a lot of these records stored within a file, 1Kb of data is starting to seem quite small. It is for these reasons that today we have storage devices that are measured in gigabytes. In order to help organise such storage devices related files are kept in folders or directories. If the files can grow quite large, then these directories can be even larger.

caution!

A record may be quite empty with many of the fields left blank or not totally filled, yet the storage space for this record can still be as great as one totally filled. This is because the computer's filing system will reserve the same space for each record whether all the fields are full or not. This can seem like wasted space, but that is the way it is. If a field is declared as being 50 characters long then space for 50 characters is reserved even if they are not all used. Good initial design can overcome some of this waste.

3.2. Types of Memory

Memory is divided into two main types, ROM and RAM. Both are types of electronic components contained within the computer's base unit.

ROMs contain programs and data that are written into them at the time of manufacture. The data and programs can be read and used by the computer, but not altered in any way. This is read only. There is a ROM inside the computer that 'wakes up' the system when the computer is first switched on. It checks the computer's own components to make sure they are working properly. It is responsible for loading other aspects of the system that then largely take over. This process is referred to as 'booting up', the action of the computer 'pulling itself up by its bootstraps'. ROMs contain important data that ensures the system runs smoothly. When power is removed the data in a ROM is not lost.

RAM is the main memory. The microprocessor will use RAM to both read data from and write data to. Data may be taken from RAM, altered by the processing that then takes place and stored back into memory. Parts of the operating system are copied into RAM when the computer is switched on. Application programs are initially loaded into RAM when they are selected for use. Whilst the program is being executed, the work you produce is also stored in RAM. RAM is measured in Mb. PCs today will have a minimum of 32 Mb of RAM, a more common value being 128Mb. PCs can have much more RAM installed. It is the need for the software to function adequately that can influence the amount of RAM necessary. Windows 98 will function with 32 Mb of RAM, but, if a memory intensive program is run from within Windows 98 then a user may wish to install more RAM.

RAM is said to be volatile. When the power is removed from a computer all the work you have done since you last saved your work will be lost! Remember to save your work at regular intervals. Data loss in the event of a power cut can be minimised with the use of an uninterruptible power supply or UPS. This is basically a device containing a battery and if a power failure occurs, the battery supplies enough power to enable any open files to be saved and the computer can be closed down properly without the loss of any data.

Cache memory is a form of RAM that is very fast but expensive in comparison to ordinary RAM. It is measured in kilobytes, Kb, rather than megabytes, Mb. 128 Kb of cache is a typical size. Cache memory is situated between the processor and main memory and is used to store frequently used or recently used program instructions. As access to this cache is much faster than access to main memory computer performance is enhanced.

Computer memory is referred to as primary or main storage. Secondary storage covers all other forms of storage such as disks and tapes. All can be generally termed auxiliary storage.

The main type of storage medium used at the present time is the disk. Hard disks with a capacity in the order of gigabytes are usually located within the computer's base unit and are used to store the operating system and the application programs. Hard drives are in-built into a computer system when new. Additional hard drives can be added to give greater storage area supplementing the original drive. Hard drives are not portable devices, although there are some available that are external devices that plug into the computer in the same way a printer will. Programs, or at least parts of them, will be loaded into RAM from the hard drive for use by the microprocessor. Some programs will set up temporary files on the hard drive whilst the program is running and erase them when the program is shut down. Hard disks are slower to access by the computer than RAM.

Floppy disks, 3.5", are used to store work and data files on. They have a capacity of 1.44 megabytes. Floppy disks are much slower to access than hard disks. The greatest advantage of these disks is their portability. The ability to take a 3.5" floppy disk between different personal computers and be able to use it holds great appeal. As 1.44 Mb is actually quite a small storage area CD-ROMs have become more popular especially for distributing software.

At present most CDs are ROMs, they can only be read from and you cannot store any additional data on them. They are said to be WORM devices, Written Once and Read Many times. However, we ought to simply refer to them as CDs now that recordable and re-writeable CDs are becoming more popular. Recordable CDs can be written to once and then read many times. A re-writeable CD can be written, and over written many times. The capacity of most CDs is around 650 megabytes. There are larger capacity CDs available that are 700Mb. CDs can be accessed more quickly than floppy disks but they are slower than hard disks. CDs are of course very portable devices. CD drives are rated in different speeds, x4, x8, x24 or x40 for example. These speeds relate to audio speed. In computing data needs to be read much faster than for reproducing audio. x4 means 4 times faster than audio speed.

A more recent innovation has been the DVD drive, (Digital Versatile Disk). These are high capacity CD-ROM discs that can store up to 17Gb of data. The latest discs have two layers and the drives use two different lasers each with a different focal length to read each of the layers. Each layer holds 4.7Gb of data. It is therefore said that a dual sided, dual density disc will hold approximately 17Gb of data. Such discs are used to store whole feature length films. Some drives are able to write to such discs, but this technology is not yet widely used. Some DVD drives that can write to such discs can only be read back on similar drives. Computers today are being sold with dual CD-ROM and DVD drives. DVD technology seems destined to be popular and to a great extent has already replaced videotape.

Tape or data cartridges can also be used to store data. These have large storage capacities but they can be slow to access the data. They cannot go directly to data as on a disc. The tape is very similar to audio tape but of a much higher quality as they need to be accelerated and decelerated at much higher speeds in order to try and improve access time. To access just two or three records on a tape can mean a great deal of winding and rewinding. Tape drives are used to backup or to archive large amounts of data, where access might only be necessary in an emergency or on a rare planned interval. They would be used on a more frequent basis in instances where there is a 'high hit rate' in such as payroll calculation.

definition

Hit rate: A calculation of the proportion of the records accessed. One would expect that for a payroll there would be a high hit rate.

Zip drives are another example of a high capacity yet portable storage medium. Zip disks are a little larger and heavier than 3.5" floppies but have a capacity of 100Mb up to 250Mb. They have gained in popularity and have been included in many personal computer systems either as an internal device or something that can be plugged in when needed.. They are not as portable as CDs or floppy disks as there are just not that many of the drives around. The advent of the DVD drive may have sealed their fate. They are mainly used for backup and archive functions, not something one would constantly run programs from.

3.3. Computer Performance

There are many factors that influence a computer's performance. We have already mentioned one of them, the availability of cache memory. The performance of a computer is judged on such factors as how quickly and efficiently an application runs, and, how long it takes to save a file to memory and to hard disk. If the computer is to be used for graphic intensive work the quality of the display and how quickly it is refreshed are key considerations. These type of criteria are often termed 'benchmarks' and are used to compare one system with another. Such comparisons can be found in many popular computer magazines.

The type of microprocessor has an obvious effect on the overall performance. A 600MHz processor is going to out perform a 166MHz processor. Other considerations are:

● More RAM generally improves the performance of a PC as it can pre-load more program code into memory where it can be accessed more quickly. Having constantly to go back to the hard disk drive for more code slows down a system.

● The type of hard drive fitted can effect the system performance. Hard drives have a stated access time. This is the time taken from when a signal is issued to read data from the drive to when data has been reliably read. Access times are stated in milliseconds, msec, with typical values of current drives being between 7 and 11 msec. This may not sound much but with frequent access and a microprocessor running at megahertz, then a few milliseconds can seem like a lifetime. Using a hard drive that is nearly full to its capacity can affect performance. Popular operating systems like Windows create a temporary file on the hard drive to help it whilst it is running. This file is deleted when Windows is closed down. If there is not enough free hard drive space then a file of less than optimum size will be created meaning more time consuming passing of data.

● When running more than one program at once, referred to as 'multi-tasking', the performance of a PC can visibly suffer. The more programs that are run at the same time, the greater the decrease in performance. The computer needs to remember where it was up to in the program that it was running so that it can pick it back up cleanly as well as the data it was using. All of this is intensive in terms of memory usage.

- A powerful graphics card will improve computer performance by displaying the screen contents more quickly and clearly. These are specialised cards that today have their own type of processor and memory on board. This relieves some of the burden off the main processor and memory. With graphic intensive programs these will provide a distinct improvement.

Simply addressing one of these components will not make a computer seem to speed along, what is required is a balance between all of them. It is no use having a 850MHz processor struggling with 16Mb of memory. It will simply spend most of its potential transferring data from disk to memory. Likewise a particularly slow hard drive can cause a bottleneck in an otherwise well specified system.

Summary

Computers are digital devices. They work with data that is represented as '0' and '1'. The binary number system is used to make working with these qualities easier. A single binary digit is called a bit, 8 bits are a byte and 4 bits a nibble.

Each memory location is capable of holding a byte of data, 8 bits, and must be given a discrete address. 1024 different memory locations are termed 1 Kilobyte, Kb, of memory. 1 Megabyte of memory, or storage space, is equal to 1,048,576 bytes. 1 Gigabyte of storage is equal to 1,073,741,824 bytes.

A character is represented by a byte of data. All of the data in a field can occupy many bytes. A record consists of many fields. All such records would be stored together in a file that would necessarily occupy many more bytes, reasonably in the region of perhaps Kb if not Mb. A directory storing all related files could occupy a considerable amount of space.

Primary or main storage is the computer memory. Secondary storage covers all other forms of storage such as disks and tapes.

There are two main types of memory ROM and RAM. ROM is read only and contains programs and data that are written into them at the time of manufacture. RAM forms the computer's main memory and can be both read from and written to. Copies of programs are written into RAM from where they can be accessed by the microprocessor. RAM is volatile and any data that is not saved will be lost when power is removed.

Cache memory is fast RAM that is situated between the processor and main memory with the main purpose of improving computer performance.

Disks are a common form of storage medium. Hard drives have a large capacity and are quick to access. They are not generally portable. 3.5" Floppy disks are used to store work and data files on and are highly portable devices. They have a capacity of 1.44 megabytes. Floppy disks are much slower to access than hard disks.

CDs are usually read only devices with a capacity of either 650Mb or 700Mb. However increasingly they are also available as writeable and re-writeable devices. DVD discs hold approximately 17Gb of data and are similar in nature to CDs.

Tape or data cartridges are also used to store data. They have large storage capacities but are slow to access the data. Tape drives are used to backup or to archive large amounts of data. Zip drives are also used for backup and archive functions. They have a capacity of 100Mb up to 250Mb and are quite portable.

Computer performance depends upon the type of microprocessor, the amount of RAM installed, the type of hard drive and type of graphics card fitted. Optimum performance can be gained from achieving the correct balance of components.

Exercises

1. Explain the terms bit and byte. How are these terms related to a character and a field?

2. Explain how main memory (RAM) and secondary storage are used for the storage of programs.

3. A well-meaning friend advises you on how to improve your computer performance. They suggest:
a) Installing more RAM.
b) Installing a faster processor.
c) Changing the type of mouse used.
d) Reducing the number of programs running at any one time.

Which courses of action do you think might help and which would not?

4. Briefly describe three different secondary storage devices stating a typical application, an advantage and a disadvantage.

Software

- *Understand the difference between application and system software.*

- *Understand the functions of an operating system.*

- *Be aware of the term Graphical User Interfaces and the advantages of such interfaces.*

- *Be aware of the common software applications together with their uses.*

- *Understand how computer systems are developed.*

4.1. Types of Software

Software is the name given to a set of instructions, or programs, that can be run on a computer. There are two types of software, systems software and application software. System software is concerned with controlling the operation of the computers hardware. Application software is any program that has been written to do a particular job, i.e. calculate a company payroll, manipulate text, etc. Both types of software will interact with each other in order to complete useful work.

4.2. Operating System Software

The most important type of system software is the operating system itself. This software loads automatically when the computer is switched on. It controls all of the hardware and ensures that the different components work with each other. The operating system will, for example, check for the presence of a keyboard when the computer is first switched on. The operating system provides an interface between the user, the applications, and the computer's hardware.

Examples of operating systems are:

MSDOS;
Windows 3.1;
Windows 95;
Windows 98;
Windows 2000;
Windows NT;
Linux;
IBM OS/2.

Most of the tasks an operating system performs are invisible to the user; for example, when a key is typed on the keyboard it displays the correct character on the monitor. If the operating system fails to load then the computer cannot be used. The number of tasks that the operating system will perform varies depending on the size and power of the computer. The operating system of a large mainframe computer, that may have to look after hundreds of users as well as the communication links between them, will be different to the operating system of a typical personal computer that may only be dealing with one user and a single communication link. Having said this the tasks that they perform are quite similar in many ways.

Some tasks carried out by an operating system are:

● Allocating internal memory (RAM).
● Transferring programs and data between disk and RAM.
● Controlling input and output devices.
● 'Booting up' the computer.
● Checking and controlling user access to prevent unauthorised access.
● Logging of errors.

There are different types of operating systems, and software bought for one operating system may not run on another. Different operating systems offer different user interfaces.

definition

> **User Interface: The way in which the user communicates with the computer. This includes both the hardware and software. A certain type of operating software will provide a certain interface.**

The first IBM personal computers came with MS DOS, Microsoft Disk Operating System. This is typified by a black screen, a C prompt and a flashing cursor awaiting a command to be typed by the user:

C:\> _

This is not very user friendly as the user has to remember a whole range of commands in order to achieve anything, (that is anything other than, "Bad command or filename".) In order to run a program the user needs to know the name of the applications file and then type this in correctly. There are other commands that need to be learnt, for example, to view the contents of a directory stopping each time the screen is full, one would type dir /p. For some users remembering all of these commands and their actual syntax is not easy. This type of operating system is often referred to as a command line interface'.

Today it is more common for personal computers to use a version of the Microsoft Windows operating system. These are graphical user interfaces, GUI's, (pronounced Gooey). These systems use a combination of pictures, (icons) and menus in order to run programs and achieve certain tasks. A mouse is useful to navigate through such systems, although not essential. They are sometimes referred to as a WIMP environment as they utilise Windows, Icons, Menus and Pointer.

Figure 4.1 Example of the Microsoft Windows graphical user interface.

The advantage of such operating systems is that all programs are run in exactly the same way and once a user has learned to perform a task within one application they can usually perform it within another. All Windows type applications have the same look and feel about them. All of the menus are arranged in the same order and often contain the same commands. By becoming proficient with one application, a user can be partly proficient in another. The user develops what is known as 'transferable skills'.

GUI's were the first environment that allowed users of personal computers to multitask – being able to run different applications in separate windows at the same time. This enables users to more easily copy data between applications. GUIs need a more capable machine to be able to run. People that are competent with a command line interface sometimes criticise GUIs for being slow and cumbersome.

The term system software also includes what are termed, 'drivers'. These are programs that are related to a certain piece of hardware, such as a certain brand of CD drive or a certain printer, ensuring that they run with a particular operating system. There can be many different drivers for a single hardware device, perhaps one driver for each of three versions of operating system, for example. If you wish to use a certain device, then you must ensure that the driver that is being supplied is for the operating system you intend to use it under.

4.3. Applications Software

Applications software is the term applied to any program that has been written to do a particular job, i.e. calculate a company payroll, manipulate text, or produce a drawing etc. Applications software is usually broken down into two sections: general purpose or generic applications software, and specialised applications software. These applications can only be run once the operating system has successfully loaded.

Generic or general-purpose applications software not only includes word processing, database, and spreadsheets, but packages such as desktop publishing, graphic packages, and presentation packages.

Word Processing Packages

 These are used to produce documents such as letters, reports, books and articles. Today's more powerful computers with increased memory have allowed modern word processing packages to include many extra features that may not have been present in earlier packages. Perhaps the greatest advantage of such a package is that the document can also be saved on disk for future amendment or use.

A modern word processing package will allow a user to:

- Type, correct, delete and move text.
- Change font size, align text left, right or centre, set tabs, set italics and bold.
- Find and replace text.
- Insert graphics and wrap text around them.
- Check spelling and grammar.
- Set up templates with type styles for different types of document.
- Work in tables or columns.
- Add headers and footers to each page.
- Create indexes and tables of contents.
- Type equations with maths symbols.
- Mail merge to send personalised letters to people selected from a list.

Spreadsheet Packages

Spreadsheets are used to store and manipulate tables of numerical data. Text, data and formulae can be entered so that the data is automatically calculated and can be recalculated if it is altered. They are ideal for storing, calculating and displaying numerical information.

One of the most useful features of a spreadsheet is its ability to perform "What If" calculations. Spreadsheets are often used in financial modelling. They are used extensively by such people as accountants, bank staff, engineers, and financial planners.

A modern spreadsheet package will allow a user to:

● Contain many related sheets within a workbook.
● Enter and copy complex formulae.
● Set up several different types of graphs.
● Use predefined mathematical functions.
● Record and create macros.
● Allow extensive formatting.
● Allow data to be filtered according to multiple criteria.
● Trace sources of error.

Database Packages

Databases are used for the storage and retrieval of information. Database programs, or Database Management Systems (DBMS) as they are called, are extremely powerful. These packages allow users to set up tables of data and to link them together. These sets of linked data can then be searched according to certain criteria stipulated by the user. More sophisticated packages will include Wizards to help the user set up the database, import data from other packages and customise the database to hide the workings of the package from an inexperienced user.

A few examples of database applications are:

● Details of the books held in a library giving author, title and subject of each book, allowing books of a particular interest to be found.
● Names and addresses of a firm's customers sorted by location and interest.
● Details of the items stored in a warehouse, giving location, cost, number currently in stock and supplier. Items below a stock reorder level can be highlighted.
● Details of students enrolled at a college. Class lists and tutor groups are generated from this information.

Desktop Publishing (DTP)

Desktop publishing allows the user to layout a page exactly as he or she wants it. They allow the entry of text, diagrams, and photographs in a variety of formats. It is easy to change fonts and write in columns, and to draw simple diagrams. Often a document is prepared using a word processor and then imported into a DTP package where it can be put into columns, different typefaces used, or diagrams added. Text is placed in boxes that can be positioned virtually anywhere on the page. Text from one box can be made to flow into another. Complex pictures and graphics can be prepared in other specialised drawing packages and then imported onto the page before printing.

caution!

The edges are now becoming a little blurred between powerful word processing packages and some of the less expensive DTP packages.

Graphics Packages

These packages are used to produce artwork. Images can be imported from and stored in a variety of formats, reflected, rotated and reduced or expanded in size. Parts of an image, or the whole image, can be copied and pasted into other locations. Contrast and brightness can be altered and the colours can be edited. Some graphics packages include specialist libraries consisting of pre-drawn images that can be imported into the package to form part of the main artwork. Images can often be input directly using a scanner. These packages are used by a wide variety of people from artists and animators to architects and engineers.

Presentation Packages

These packages are used for presenting information to an audience. They allow for the inputting of text, numerical data, graphs, and images along with the use of basic animation effects and sound. They allow for quite extensive formatting usually coming with some standard templates for the user to customise if they wish. The presentation is constructed on a number of slides. The resulting presentation can be shown in a variety of formats. The presentation can be run full-screen on a computer system with automated or remote progression through the slides. Alternatively the slides can be printed on to OHP transparencies with a set of speaker's notes produced separately.

★ ECDL ★

In the past few years many integrated packages have been produced. These are often called 'suites' or 'works'. An integrated package contains several generic programs, probably a word processor, a graphics package, database, communications (e-mail) software and spreadsheet. Examples include Microsoft Office, Lotus Smart Suite, Microsoft Works and Claris Works. All the component parts have the same 'look and feel' and it is very easy to transfer data from one function to another. These integrated packages can prove to be more economical than purchasing each package separately if one intends to use each of the individual packages.

Specialised applications software is designed to carry out a specific task, sometimes for a particular industry. It is of little use in other situations. Examples include payroll processing, timetabling and attendance monitoring. With the rise in computers within the home there has been an increase in specialist software to support a wide variety of interests. These include family tree programs, menu planners, flight simulators, route planners, maps and city guides.

Application software that is not bought 'off the shelf' but written especially for a user is called bespoke or tailor-made software. Bespoke software can either be developed in-house, by programmers employed by the user's company, or by using an outside agency.

Multimedia is software that can combine the use of text, sound, video, animation and graphics. The user of a multimedia encyclopaedia, for example, can search for information on say, "Martin Luther King"; not only can they read about his life, but see video sequences and hear his voice if they wish. Multimedia is often used in Training and Education, Information and Marketing, and Entertainment. Multimedia has become synonymous with the term CBT, Computer Based Training. The potential for interactivity with such software makes it the perfect tool for developing resource based learning packages.

Such packages are constructed using multimedia-authoring packages. The developer can specify the flow of the material and the level of interactivity along with feedback given to the user. Text, graphics, sound, video, and animation can all be imported within such a package. When the developer is happy with the final version a separate package can be compiled that can be run independently of the authoring software.

The advantages of multimedia are that it is seen to be more varied and flexible than a book. It is interactive, a person can learn by doing, not just listening or reading. Specific feedback on certain actions can be given. Multimedia presented on a CD can contain huge volumes of information and the power of the computer can be used to search through it in a non-laborious fashion. The user can usually take a variety of paths through the material. The path need not be linear. A more experienced person can be speeded through sections whilst a less experienced user given the support needed.

However, along with the advantages there are also disadvantages to be considered. There is a need for special equipment that can be quite expensive, which is obviously not the case with a book. Reading large amounts from a screen can be tiring. People working within an office environment will often print off memos e-mailed to them rather than read them on screen. Unless a portable PC is available, you cannot take it to bed, on holiday, on the bus etc. There is more material available in book form than on CD and since the book has a considerable advantage in terms of development time, this is likely to be the case for sometime.

Every few years a new version of the same software package is produced that takes advantage of increased speed, memory and the processing power of later computers. Each version has a number such as Excel 97, PageMaker 6, or Word 95. New versions will offer new facilities in an attempt to get users to upgrade. Excel 2 has no graph wizard. Excel 3 does. Excel 3 has no spell check. Excel 4 does. Excel 5 offers two sorts of macros. These version numbers can be a little confusing. The '.0' versions (4.0, 5.0) are usually major up-grades from the previous versions. Minor changes are then incorporated in later .1 or .2 versions.

Work produced on an earlier version should be useable on later ones, although it is rarely true the other way round. For example, all data produced in WordPerfect 5.1 can be used in WordPerfect 6.1, but not vice versa. This is referred to as 'backwards compatibility.'

4.4. Systems Development

A computer system may be changed for a number of reasons. It may be that the current system is no longer suitable for its intended

purpose. Originally it may have been fine, but changes in working practices or expansion of a business can render a system less than ideal. The technology used may have become out of date. A company may wish to take advantage of new services offered by the latest technology such as on-line ordering and payment.

There are recognised stages in the development of a computer-based system. A systems analyst would be heavily involved in the initial stages. Firstly research would be carried out into the problem or situation for which the software is required. A feasibility study would be undertaken to see if it is technically and economically possible to complete the work within the required timescale and the specified costs.

If it were decided to continue with the project the systems analyst would produce a specification for the project to be constructed against. The software would then be written. Once written it would be tested to ensure that it meets the prescribed specification.

Software producers need to demand very high standards for the testing of software. No one would want to purchase a less than perfect product. The people testing the system should try to deliberately make it fail in some way. It is vitally important to discover any serious shortcomings in the new system before it is released. Colleagues who have not been involved with the actual production themselves should test a program in-house. This is often termed alpha testing. The next stage would be to release the software to selected users to test out and report bugs before the final release date. This is termed beta testing. This gives the developers the opportunity to test the software on different hardware. Differences in microprocessors, memory size and sound and video cards for example, can all affect software performance. The developers would receive feedback on this performance.

An evaluation report would be produced on the performance and limitations of the new system or software.

Summary
There are two types of software, systems software and application software. System software is concerned with controlling the operation of the computer hardware. Application software is any program that has been written to do a particular job

Examples of system software are the various versions of Windows, MSDOS, Linux, and IBM OS/2. Hardware drivers are examples of systems software that relate to the particular functioning of a hardware device.

Today most operating systems provide a graphical user interface, a GUI.

If the operating system fails to load then the computer cannot be used. The operating system will interact with the applications that run on the system.

Applications software packages include word processing, spreadsheet, database, desktop publishing, graphics and presentation packages.

An integrated package contains several generic programs. These can prove to be more economical that purchasing each package separately if one intends to use each of the individual packages. Data should be more easily transferred between the different elements of an integrated package.

Many specialist software packages exist, written to fulfil a specific specialist need. Bespoke software is tailor made software written perhaps for a particular company for a certain purpose.

Multimedia is software that can combine the use of text, sound, video, animation and graphics. Multimedia software has the advantage of being capable of offering a highly interactive medium.

The processes of research, analysis, development, testing and evaluation are all involved in the development of computer based systems.

Software needs to be extensively tested. This testing may involve both testing in-house, termed alpha testing, and testing outside of the company on a wide variety of systems by selected people, termed beta testing.

Exercises

1. Explain the difference between systems software and applications software stating an example of each.

2. Name an advantage of both a GUI and a command line interface.

3. Give three functions of an operating system.

4. Briefly describe three application packages and state a typical use.

5. List three tasks you can accomplish easily on a word processor that you could not easily do on a typewriter.

6. State three advantages of presenting learning using multimedia and one possible disadvantage.

7. During the development of a software package state the purpose of beta testing.

Information Networks

In this chapter you will learn how to

- *Understand the definitions of Local Area Networks and Wide Area Networks.*

- *Know reasons for using a network.*

- *Understand the use of the telephone network in computing.*

- *Understand the term electronic mail and know its possible uses.*

- *Understand the concept of the Internet and its uses.*

5.1. LAN and WAN

Many computers do not stand alone but are connected to others for the purpose of communication in what is termed a network. It is impossible to ignore computer networks in our daily life. They are in the smallest of offices to the largest of businesses, and with the advent of the Internet, they are truly worldwide. With such wide usage there are significant benefits to be had:

● In order to share work many people will swap data on portable storage media, such as a 3.5" floppy disk. Sharing work files across a network is easy and efficient, and doesn't have the restriction of file sizes imposed by the floppy disk.

● There can often be bottlenecks when more than one person needs access to information. Letting more than one person have access to a database at one time can improve productivity. If there is a lot of data to be manually entered into a database then shared access has an obvious advantage. As long as controls are put into place, this type of sharing can be achieved efficiently whilst at the same time maintaining the integrity of the data.

● Printers and other expensive peripheral devices that are not always in constant use can be shared. Each computer does not need to have an individual printer attached. Access to expensive peripherals, such as a colour laser printer, can be granted to many users.

● Telecommunication services can be accessed and shared. Sharing a modem between many users avoids the need to purchase multiple units.

● Security of access and of data files can be improved with the implementation of different levels of passwords with different access rights.

LAN or WAN? Networks are classified according to the number of users they support and the size of the area they cover. There can, however, be a lot of confusion in categorising some networks as there are no hard and fast rules that make the categories distinct. The two broad categories are LAN and WAN. A Local Area Network, (LAN) is often defined as one where the users are relatively close together, within a single room, floor, or building. A Wide Area Network, (WAN) is one that covers a wider geographical area, connecting computers that maybe be quite remote.

Sometimes it is hard to distinguish between the two: some LAN's span more than one building, and some networks that span more than one building are termed a WAN! The key to being able to distinguish between the two is to consider the medium by which they communicate. A LAN will communicate by 'normal' network cable, since the distances can be physically small, thus enabling a direct connection to be made. WANs involve the use of a range of connection methods including the telephone system and communication satellites. Satellite communications are now fairly common and provide a better alternative medium for transmission across oceans than undersea cable.

It can be easier to think of networks in terms of the number of users. A small LAN with between 5 to 50 users that does not employ any dedicated IT staff is termed a workgroup. The next level is an intermediate or departmental LAN serving up to around 200 users. These would be corporate networks installed within a large sized company. Joining workgroups together could make a departmental LAN. An enterprise network will serve around 500 users spread across multiple offices, floors or buildings. There are other names that crop-up when talking about computer networks such as campus networks installed within academic institutions.

The topology of a network is a description, diagrammatically, of how the cabling is laid out and the manner in which the terminals are connected to this cabling. The three most commonly used topologies, shown in Figure 5.1, are Bus, Ring and Star. In a Bus network the terminals are connected in a line with a single data packet travelling between the various points on the network to its destination. Unfortunately if the line is broken at any point then the terminals in each split section are isolated from the others.

definition

Data Packet: Data travels around a network split up into small parcels called packets. Each packet is divided into discrete sections known as fields. Each network packet can be different, but there are some common fields. Most have start and end fields, containing information relating to the source and destination for the data, the length of the data being sent, and a field to enable error checking.

Bus Ring Star

Network topologies

Figure 5.1 Examples of common networking topologies.

This situation is overcome to some extent by joining the ends of the line together as in a Ring network. If more than one connection is broken then terminals can still become isolated.

The Star network is used extensively in modern networks. The terminals are all connected to a central hub that reads the data packets received and forwards them to the correct destination. The advantage of such a topology is that if a fault develops, then only the terminal attached to the hub via that connection is affected leaving the rest of the network unaffected. Such networks can run up quite an expensive cabling bill.

Two other terms that need to be explained at this stage are "client-server" and "peer to peer." A networked computer that has information that other computers want to access is called a server. A computer that wants to access this information is called a client. Client-server networks operate on the assumption that the workstations on a network want to access applications, files, and storage areas that are located centrally on a dedicated computer, or file server. Most LANs will use single or multiple servers. Security and access is much easier to manage on a client-server system.

Peers to peer networks are constructed under the assumption that all computers attached to the network are equal. Each computer acting both as a client and a server is attached to each of the others. Windows for Workgroups, Windows 95, 98 and 2000 editions all have the capability to offer peer to peer networking. A computer on such a network will be able to share its files, printers, and modem with other computers. There is no need to employ an expensive server with such a system. Peer to peer networks tend to function slower than client-server networks. If one computer is turned off then all the devices and data concerned with the computer are unavailable to the rest.

5.2. The Telephone Network in Computing

Without the use of the public telephone system WANs would be very limited. In order to communicate across any appreciable distance it is not practical to install network cables, especially when an adequate alternative already exists.

PSTN, PSDN and ISDN

The telephone network has over the years has undergone a series of metamorphoses, much of which has been invisible to the user. The Public Switched Telephone Network (PSTN) was originally designed for voice transmission, using analogue electrical signals. A telephone mouthpiece functions like a speaker in reverse. It contains a diaphragm that vibrates when struck by sound waves. These vibrations are converted into electrical signals that are sent over the network.

In electronics there are actually two quite distinct fields, one dealing with digital signals and one dealing with analogue signals. A digital signal is one that is seen to be physically in one state or its opposite, at one of two opposite extremes. These states are represented by the binary digits 1 and 0. They are usually represented by a square wave. A switch or and LED indicator could be seen as digital devices..

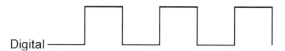

Digital

Figure 5.2 Example of a digital signal.

Analogue signals can be at either extreme or at any value in-between. Such signals are usually represented with a sine wave. Our senses for heat, light and sound function in an analogue fashion.

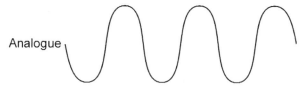

Analogue

Figure 5.3 Example of an analogue signal.

Many people are surprised to learn that the telephone system actually handles more data traffic than voice traffic. This has led to the establishment of a Public Switched Data Network (PSDN). Much of the main network is now geared up to work with digital traffic. The analogue connections are mainly confined to local links to homes and businesses.

Further to the development of this digital network is the Integrated Services Digital Network line, (ISDN). Such lines are designed to carry a variety of digitised data all integrated into a single connection. They are designed specifically for the integrated transmission of text, sound, graphics and video. Such connections are wholly digital and provide for fast and reliable transmission. It is hoped that the use of ISDN lines will provide a global network with common standards.

 In the UK a dedicated line can be leased from British Telecom and provide a permanent connection for devices in a network. Users are charged a flat rate for the lease of the line no matter how much or how little it is used. They are cost-effective if there is a need for a permanent connection or for high volume data transmission.

Most people use a 'dial-up' line from home. A home Internet connection is often referred to as a 'dial-up connection.' These are cheaper, but are not as fast as leased lines.

Broadcast Technology

Communication networks also include broadcast technologies such as those used by television, radio broadcasting, and cellular telephone systems.

Database services are provided by television and are collectively known as Teletext. The BBC Teletext service is known as Ceefax and ITV has Oracle. To access these services a television receiver must have a Teletext decoder. Teletext consists of simple text pages that the viewer can access via the television remote control.

Cellular telephone networks use cellular radio communications operating in the UHF (ultra-high frequency) band. Local base stations allow cellphone users to access the PSTN. Each base station covers a cell site, an area within which it can pick up cellphone signals. Although the signals can penetrate buildings and other barriers a user must be within a few miles of a transmitter. It is for this reason that the growing popularity of cellular phones has been accompanied with a similar rise in the number of transmitters.

WAP (Wireless Application Protocol) is designed by the mobile telecommunication industry to allow mobile phone users access to basic Internet functions. It is a global standard that is a combination of a communication protocol and an application. As it is difficult to view a standard Internet page on a mobile phone, WAP pages are pared down equivalents. By no means all Internet pages are yet WAP compatible.

Connecting to a Communications Network

To transmit computer data over analogue sections of the PSTN requires use of a modem. Modems are used to connect a computer to a dial-up line. The term modem comes from the fact that it is used to "modulate " and "demodulate" the signals that are transmitted over the PSTN. This functions in much the same way as normal radio signals. To listen to a radio station we tune in to the carrier frequency that has been modulated with the signal of the music or voice transmitted. The carrier frequency gives the signals the power to be transmitted – it carries them. A radio will demodulate this signal removing the carrier frequency so that the music and voice can be heard.

In terms of computer data, two different frequencies are used to represent the digital 1's and 0's. These frequencies, in the audible range, can be transmitted in the usual fashion over the PSTN. When receiving data the modem will demodulate the two frequencies into the 1's and 0's that the computer will understand.

The power of your personal computer does not affect too much the speed at which you can access the Internet. It is the modem speed that has most effect. The speed of a modem is specified by its baud rate. The baud rate is simply the number of bits per second that can be transmitted or received. Currently 55.6Kbps (Kilobits per second) is the fastest baud rate. A faster baud rate can save on telephone call charges as the time spent waiting to receive data will be reduced.

information

ADSL (Asymmetric Digital Subscriber Line). This technology has been developed with a view to revolutionising Internet access for the home and business user. It utilises existing copper phone lines to transmit digital data faster than modems and ISDN lines. It is termed asymmetric because the transmission rate between the phone exchange and the user is faster than the other way around. Speeds of between 512 Kilobits per second and 2 Megabits per second between home and user are being quoted. In the opposite direction the quoted speed is 256 Kilobits per second. Since most people use the Internet for downloading data it is seen as a great advantage to have the fastest speed in this direction. The connection also splits the computer digital data from the analogue voice data so that simultaneous use is possible. Internet access will no longer tie up the phone for normal voice use.

Telex and Fax

The use of Telex was quite common in the 1960's. To the user a telex machine basically consisted of a teleprinter, a kind of typewriter that could also act as a printer, connected to a phone line enabling messages to be sent instantly to another telex machine. The user would dial the receiver's telex machine and await confirmation of a connection being established. The sender could then type text messages that would be replicated immediately by the receiver's telex machine. The messages were always in uppercase letters and a hard copy was both sent and received. There were no VDU's involved.

Advancement came with the ability to key the message to punched tape prior to connection and then use the tape to speed up transmission. The teleprinter when delivering the Saturday's football results on television gave a good indication of how a telex message would be received. A telex machine was said to "combine the speed of the telephone with the authenticity of the written word." The telex machine has been overtaken by the use of the fax machine.

Fax (facsimile) machines scan a piece of paper and transmit the image as digital data via the telephone network to another fax machine. It is not text, or an actual graphic that is sent, but a representation of what is seen during scanning,

in black or white. A reconstructed black and white image emerges at the receiver. As with the telex machine, the receiver's fax number must firstly be dialled and a connection established before data transmission can be established. The great advantage over telex is the ability to send diagrams as well as text. Some modems can double as fax machines.

5.3 Electronic Mail

E-mail stands for electronic mail. E-mail provides the facility for one-to-one communication. It is used in much the same way as conventional postal mail, but the information being sent is electronic and therefore much quicker. In some respects it is similar to a fax, but there is actually no need for a hard copy (printed output) of material to be sent. E-mail users refer to conventional postal mail systems as "snail mail".

In order to send e-mail, and access the Internet, the user needs to have a computer system connected to a phone line, possibly via a modem. In addition an account with an Internet Service provider, ISP, is needed. The ISP will provide the user with mail software, such as Microsoft Outlook, Internet Software and mail facilities. At the time of sign up the user will be given an e-mail address. This e-mail address is usually in the form of 'your.name@ISPname' all in lower case letters. Each e-mail address needs to be unique and this often necessitates some alterations being made to your name, for example john.lancaster87.

To send e-mail the sender logs onto their ISP and sends their message to the ISP's mail server. The message can be text, or a simple message with a computer file, or files, attached. Once sent to the ISP the sender can forget the message as the ISP's mail facilities will take over automatically sending the mail to the receiver's e-mail server. When the receiver next logs onto their server they can download the message and read it and open any attached files.

E-mail removes the needs for the sender and receiver to actually be in direct contact with one another, only the mail servers come into contact. Mail servers are always available to send and receive mail, so mail can be sent when ready and downloaded to be read when convenient. As the connection is only from sender to ISP and receiver to ISP all transmissions for the user are completed at local call rates. The speed, relatively low cost and relative confidentiality of e-mail contrasts favourably with the use of everyday postal mail systems.

An additional advantage of e-mail is that one message can be sent to many receiving computers. There can be perhaps just a few people receiving the message, within perhaps a single organisation, or many people on an extensive mailing list. Abuse of this facility by sending unwanted material to others can cause annoyance and is termed "spamming".

5.4. The Internet

The Internet was started in the late 1960s as an experiment in the United States by the Advanced Research Projects Agency which later became the Defence Advanced Research Projects Agency. They developed the ARPAnet which was a network consisting of a small number of computers situated geographically remote from one another. The aim was to establish the feasibility of building a network that could survive in the event of a nuclear strike. Such a network must still be able to function if a number of the hosts were not working.

This successful experiment was then used by scientists to store and communicate scientific documents amongst each other. This became a popular means of sharing information and keeping abreast of new developments. Later Universities, academic institutions, and commercial organisations gained use of the technology. The Internet is actually the physical resource used to form this worldwide network. Today the Internet is a truly global network of computer networks, linking together millions of computer systems. The Internet is not run or owned by any one organisation.

During this development it became quickly apparent that there needed to be some method of linking the vast array of scientific text documents that floated on the Internet. A system of linking and finding a particular document was developed in the early 1990's called hypertext. Hypertext is simply text that when selected by a mouse click will transport the user to the destination pointed to by the hypertext link. This interface was later developed into the World Wide Web, WWW, a system that provides for easy movement from one Internet resource to another as well as a method of searching for a particular topic. The WWW is the actual software interface that allows us to search and view information held at specific 'web sites' on the Internet.

Today these web sites do not just hold pages of simple text, but they also have the capability to display pages with images, sound and video. There are many, many sites available today covering an array of subjects beyond most people's imagination. With so much information on the many sites available, finding the right information can be very difficult.

Search engines such as Yahoo, Alta Vista and Lycos enable users to search the Internet for selected key words. These search engines search the web sites available according the key words stipulated by the user. A search on one key word may provide thousands of links. The search engine will list the first set of most likely hits, possibly the top ten. Hyperlinks are provided directly to the site(s) selected.

information

The search engines mentioned above can be found on the Internet at the following addresses:

http://www.yahoo.com
http://www.altavista.com
http://www.lycos.co.uk

Although when using the Internet the user may be involved in global communication the cost is reduced to that of a local telephone call. The user is actually only connected to their ISP which is usually just a local phone call away. ISPs will often allocate to a subscriber a certain amount of web space so that they can set up their own web page for others to view.

Intranets

An Intranet is an internal network, for example, within a company or academic institution, which includes information pages and e-mail facilities. It uses the same interface as the Internet and can even provide connection to the Internet.

Summary

People use networks of computers to share files and devices, and to communicate with each other.

Networks can be broadly classified as Local Area Networks, LANs, that are a number of computers physically close to each other which are connected together, and Wide Area Networks, WANs, that cover a wide geographical area.

The topology of a network describes how the cabling is laid out and the manner in which the terminals are connected to this cabling. Common topologies are Bus, Ring and Star networks.

Client-server networks utilise a central dedicated computer serving files and resources to other computers on the network that are termed clients. Peer-to-peer networks utilise computers that act both as clients and servers with no one computer in overall control.

WANs often use the public switched telephone network, PSTN, in order to communicate across appreciable distances. This extensive use has led to the development of the public switched data network, PSDN, and integrated services digital network lines, ISDN lines, in order to speed up transmission rates.

Communication over large distances can also be achieved by satellite and radio communication.

Digital signals are in one of two physical states, at one of two opposite extremes. These states are represented by the binary digits 1 and 0. Analogue signals can be at one of these extreme states or at any value in-between.

A modem is needed to connect the digital computer to the analogue telephone lines. The speed of data transmission is measured in bits per second, bps.

One of the first devices for sending text messages between two points via the telephone network was the telex machine. Advancements were made in the form of the facsimile machine, fax, allowing both text and images to be sent.

E-mail, (electronic mail), provides the ability to communicate text and computer files between two people or from one person to many people. To use e-mail, connection to the Internet is needed together with the services of an Internet Service Provider, ISP. E-mail is sent at the rate of a local rate telephone call.

The Internet is a global network of computers. The World Wide Web provides an interface for easy location and movement between resources that are stored on the Internet. Search engines are software tools that locate resources on the Internet according to key words specified by the user.

Exercises

1. What is the difference between a LAN and a WAN?

2. State an advantage and a disadvantage of using each of the telephone, Fax, and e-mail.

3. Briefly describe the relationship between the Internet and the World Wide Web.

4. What facilities are needed to provide a user with access to the Internet?

5. Describe the difference between analogue and digital signals.

6. What is a modem used for and how is its speed specified?

Computers in Everyday Life

In this chapter you will learn how to

- *Know some of the uses of the PC at home.*
- *Know the uses of office applications.*
- *Be aware of examples of computer systems used in industry, business, government, and education.*
- *Be able to give examples of situations where a computer may be appropriately used.*
- *Be aware of the use of computers in everyday life.*

6.1. Computers in the Home

Today the computer is as common a sight in the home as it is in business and industry. The variety of uses that a home computer is put to is as wide as its use in business and industry. Different members of the household will use a home computer in different ways and it must be seen to be capable of satisfying each need.

The home computer is often used to enhance a hobby. It can be a tool for the garden enthusiast both as an information source on plants and crops and for garden design. Many different designs can be effortlessly tried along with a variety of plants. The more capable garden design software can allow the user to view the design in various stages of its life cycle displaying the projected plant growth as the garden matures.

To people studying genealogy the computer is an invaluable recording and research tool. Specialist software exists to help record a family tree in a professional manner. The ability to access documents via the Internet gives access to global information that until recently would have been impossible for many individuals. The ability to communicate with people via e-mail allows for contacts that can prove invaluable.

Indeed for many the computer has become a hobby in itself. The structure and the different possible configurations of a computer system seem to fascinate many. A computer system must be unique as a piece of electrical equipment that the user can take the top off and add or remove components without invalidating the overall warranty. For some 'surfing' the Internet holds enough fascination, whilst for many others a computer is the ultimate entertainment tool.

definition

Surfing: Searching for information on the Internet by whatever route seems interesting.

For other family members the home computer can be seen as a tool for more serious use. People with the responsibility for running a home can find a computer invaluable in helping to manage household accounts. Many people are paid a monthly salary and have bills and investments paid by such means as direct debit. Keeping track of income and outgoings can be a daunting task. Seemingly gone are the days of cash in a pay packet and queues to pay bills.

For the younger family member possibly studying a much wider curriculum than their parents, a computer becomes a valuable homework tool. With a computer's production capabilities and use of multimedia CD-ROMs, research and presentation of projects can become a fascinating endeavour rather than a laborious task. There are even specialist Web sites for that vital examination revision.

The division between work and home has become ever so fine. The development in computer technology for some can make this division indistinguishable. Teleworking, or telecommuting as it is sometimes called, has given people the opportunity to work at home via a computer linked to their office. The home computer becomes just an extended terminal on the company's network. This can be ideal for some. There is flexibility of working time and no need to provide office space, lighting and heating. It can mean the comfort of your own home to work in. There is no need, for example, for a sales person to travel into a busy city centre office to pick up documentation and then travel back the way they came to carry out their business. The documents can be downloaded at home and the day's work begun immediately. At the end of the day the documentation can be uploaded to the office without physically having to visit it. Contact with colleagues can be made by telephone, fax, or e-mail. An employer can recruit from a much wider geographical area.

For others teleworking can prove to be an unpleasant experience. The distractions of the home can prove too much. The meter reader, a salesperson, lost courier, and hungry pet can all seem larger than life distractions, (not to mention the young child home from school!).

There is the feeling of always being at work and not just because you work at home. An organised person who may be able to cope with the home environment can come up against other difficulties. Colleagues do not know your working hours and will think nothing of phoning, faxing or expecting e-mails to be read at all times of the day and night, "Sorry didn't know you were on holiday" is no comfort when a week's work has just downloaded. Teleworkers can feel pressured into over performing in an effort to keep up with office based colleagues.

Teleworkers can feel isolated from colleagues. In fact some companies will insist that workers gather in the office at a specified time of the week just to get over this feeling of isolation. This can also help to foster a sense of corporate identity and instil a sense of loyalty.

6.2. Computers at Work or in Education

Computers in the Office

The use of computer technology has changed dramatically the way in which many businesses operate. The term 'office automation' is used to express the manner in which most types of office functions are now performed using computers, or devices that rely on an in-built dedicated microprocessor. The use of hardware such as answering machines, fax machines, and photocopiers in addition to computers have changed the way office work is now performed. The aim is to improve efficiency and communication.

The introduction of such hardware at one time led people to believe that we were heading towards a paperless office. Many believe we still may be heading that way, but others believe the information processing capabilities of such devices actually create even more paper!

Offices in fact use quite a small range of general application software packages. The most commonly used are Word Processing, Spreadsheets, Databases and E-mail applications. Database systems manage recorded details of, for example, customers, suppliers, enrolments, catalogues, and appointments. The ability to interrogate such records in a flexible manner is provided by such systems. They can be relatively small with records shared between one or two workers in a small office, or, huge stores of records accessed by many workers across a wide area network from remote locations.

Computers in Business

 There are many other applications that are specially designed to help with the running and decision-making processes within business. Some of these are of use generally, others have a more specialist application:

● Accounting packages to ease the burden of financial management.

● Statistics Packages for carrying out statistical analysis of data. These can be used to help detect and predict trends.

● Management Information Systems (MIS). These systems are designed to provide the right information to the right manager at the right time. Different levels of management will require different information, perhaps in a different format, in order to be effective at

their job. This information would then be used to support a structured decision making process influencing, for example, budgets or sales targets.

● Decision Support Systems (DSS). These are integrated systems that use data from a variety of different sources. They are primarily aimed at senior managers who make strategic decisions. They utilise sophisticated data analysis techniques on an interactive basis to aid the decision making process. The information they provide may not routinely be provided by an MIS. For example, a company director may wish to know the effect on profits if the sales increase by 10% and the costs increase by 6%.

Specialist Use of Computers in Industry

Computer aided design (CAD) and computer aided manufacturing (CAM) are two terms often linked with the use of computers in industry. CAD is a general term used to refer to software packages that are used to design an artefact. Computers can be used to design the smallest mechanical component, a circuit board layout, or a shopping complex. Detailed drawings, including accurate measurements, can be produced to a fine scale in a large format.

CAM is the use of computers and other automated equipment to control the production of an artefact. Such automated production lines may not have the flexibility of skilled manual labour, but once set up they will consistently produce accurate, high quality products with little maintenance for long periods of time. CAD/CAM refers to the linking of the software design tool to the automatic production. From conception to artefact in one fell swoop!

Computers can also be used to test products and monitor the production line. These are referred to as computers, but they look very different to the one on the office desk. They are in the main microprocessor controlled systems rather than a PC.

Computers in Government

Government agencies use computers to store and interrogate vast numbers of personal records. The actual details stored will vary depending upon which country a person is living in. The minimum information a person might reasonably expect that a government agency has stored on them would be their name and address together with their social security number or a national identification number. Each time someone is involved in an activity such as paying tax or voting, details will be added to many different registers. Personal details may be stored by public administration information systems which collect information on births, deaths, marriages, criminal records, driving licence records, examination records, population census, and passport records, to name but a few.

Computers in Education

Computers are used widely in many schools, colleges and training institutions. They are used not only for common administration, recording and production purposes, but also play a role in the process of education itself.

Many tutoring packages enable the student to obtain information, ask questions and even obtain a marked score on a test. Computer Aided Learning, CAL, has many advantages. The learning material can be enriched with sound, images and video to provide a more stimulating environment. Students can work at their own pace, perhaps taking a different route through the material according to their ability. If difficulties are encountered an exercise can be repeated as many times as the user wishes without the computer getting tired or irritable. Some find the instant feedback gained from computer marked tests encouraging.

There are disadvantages of CAL and over use can serve to highlight some of these. It can be laborious reading large amounts of information from a screen. The valuable interaction between teacher and student is missing. A student cannot ask for something to be explained from a different viewpoint. A lesson cannot therefore be easily changed to suit a certain group of individuals. Some students need the discipline and motivational skills of a human teacher as well as the constraints of a set timetable.

Appropriate Use Of Computers

When we consider the vast array of activities that computers are involved in one might ask, "Is there nothing a computer cannot do?"

Computers undoubtedly have many advantages; they never get tired, frustrated, hungry or angry; they can produce an extensive range of documents that can be easily re-called and edited; they can cross-reference facts derived from many different sources.

Computers also have many disadvantages. They breakdown, (usually at the most inopportune moment), training and recruiting people to use computers can be difficult and expensive, some information systems need to be set-up and maintained by highly trained staff, and some people are fearful of computers which can cause undue stress in the workplace.

So what makes computers good for some tasks? To answer this question we need to consider the desirable attributes of a computer system. The first attribute that usually comes to mind is speed. Computers can carry out tasks at lighting speed that would take an age manually.

Consider sorting a list of thousands of names alphabetically. A computer can merge the names and addresses of hundreds of people into a standard letter in an instant. To do this manually would possible negate the job being performed at all.

Computers are very consistent in their actions. Once information is entered correctly, a computer will be process these consistently. If we consider the merged letter above, a different letter could be merged with the same names and addresses that would be sent exactly to the same names and addresses. Computers are also very accurate. Calculations are performed with great precision in a consistent manner.

caution!

> **The computer can only produce correct output if it receives correct input. Garbage in, garbage out.**

A computer and associated peripherals can hold vast amounts of information in a very small space.

Computers can carry out dangerous tasks or enter dangerous environments where humans cannot, or would prefer not to enter. They can also help provide round-the-clock service with minimal human resources performing boring and arduous tasks.

Computers are not always the answer. It can be a surprise to some people that humans are considered superior in many situations. A human is better when the situation calls for particularly 'human' touches. Humans are better when creativity is required, where judgement and experience are needed and where human feelings need to be taken into account. Humans are also adaptable and better in situations where the tasks to be performed are different each time. Could a robot cuddle a baby when it cries?

Computers – fast, accurate, stupid.

Man – slow, slovenly, smart.

6.3. Computers in Daily Life.

Computers have already had a great effect on society, an effect that is likely to increase as computers get faster and more capable. Whilst advances in computer technology are made, the price of a computer tends to remain quite static. People today are purchasing a much more technologically advanced and capable computer for about the same price as they were ten years ago. The use of computers can be seen in many walks of daily life.

Computers in Shops

Computers are used in shops and supermarkets to help provide a better service to the customer. Some of their uses are obvious to the customer some are not so apparent. The use of barcodes has many advantages for the customer and the retailer.

information

A barcode consists of a unique combination of vertical parallel lines of different thickness together with a numeric code that is printed onto a product's packaging. Barcode readers, seen at supermarket checkouts, use optical methods to scan the bar codes. From this barcode each product is identified and its price automatically entered at the till from information held on the central computer. Barcodes are a very easy and cost-effective way of inputting data. The central computer can record every item sold and therefore help with stock control.

Barcodes enable the cost to the customer to be quickly entered and therefore help reduce queuing in addition to providing a much more detailed receipt. However on the occasions when the barcode and associated number is damaged or is not recognised, delays can occur.

For the retailer, prices of goods can be more easily changed. The price code is changed at the central computer eliminating the need to replace many conventional printed tags on individual products. This can be a little frustrating for the customer as it is not always made clear exactly what they will be charged.

Today credit cards, plastic cards with a magnetic strip containing the users PIN or Personal Identification Number together with their account number, are widely used instead of cash to purchase goods and services. A credit card is 'swiped', or passed through a special reader, using a communications link to automatically dial up and check the cards credit status and verify that it has not expired or been reported as lost or stolen.

Credit cards are considered safer than carrying large amounts of cash around. People use them as they are more widely accepted than personal cheques and often carry a level of basic insurance on the goods purchased. However, not all retailers accept them, as many smaller operations do not have the means to process them. Retailers prefer them as they can check a customer's credit rating rather then take a chance on a cheque. Many types of credit cards can be used in different countries eliminating the need to carry foreign cash. This convenience must be balanced against the temptation to overspend and the high interest rates charged on outstanding balances.

In order to improve the security and flexibility of cards that carry a magnetic strip holding the information, smart cards have been developed. These cards are the same size as credit cards but have a microprocessor sealed inside them to replace the magnetic strip. As well as holding much more data they can also encrypt this data making it unintelligible to an unauthorised person. They are widely used today in satellite television decoders to ensure the user has paid the necessary subscription for the channels received.

Computers and Banking

Computers are an integral part of banking. Some people only encounter a bank's computer when using the automatic cash machines. These are referred to as ATMs or Automatic Teller Machines and can be used for viewing statements and withdrawing cash. In fact the use of a bank's computer system is far more widespread.

All the transactions that take place in relation to a particular account are recorded by the use of a computer. Keeping up-to-date with currency rates and share prices that constantly change is important to financial houses.

It is also possible to bank from home directly via the telephone or the Internet. It is possible to arrange to pay your bills, order chequebooks, and view your balance. This can be done at any time of the day or night and is not dependent on banking hours. Security is obviously a worry, but banks use software that is very sophisticated and the way that the data is encrypted during transmission makes on-line banking arguably more secure than any other type of banking.

Computers in Libraries

Library services make extensive use of computers for both library administration and presentation of information. Library books can be given a bar code that incorporates an ISBN. The ISBN is an International Standard Book Number that enables the title, author and where and when the book was printed to be established. Library cards now contain bar codes that can be read by a scanner. Combining the book's bar code and the borrower's library card code enables easy tracking of loans. Information on who has borrowed the book, when the book will be returned, and whether or not it has been reserved for another borrower, can all be retrieved.

Many libraries are linked to a national network enabling inter-library loans. Books can have a magnetic security tag that has to be deactivated before the book can be borrowed preventing books from being stolen.

Computers in the Doctor's Surgery

Today a doctor who is a general practitioner may practice from within a medical centre along with a number of other doctors. Such large practices cater for the needs of a large number of patients. Computers are being used to help medical centres manage their information. Even the smallest practice finds a computer system invaluable.

Computers can be used to store, retrieve and update patient records. Many medical records updated in this fashion do not allow for deletion of details removing any suspicion of malpractice.

Computers can prove an invaluable source of information for the doctor themselves. Access to drug databases, reference materials, and current medical advances can all help in keeping a doctor informed of global developments.

Summary

Today the computer is a common sight in the home and is put to a variety of uses. Different members of the household will use a home computer in different ways. The computer is often used to enhance a hobby.

For other family members the home computer can be seen as a tool for more serious use. People with the responsibility for running a home can find a computer invaluable in helping to manage household accounts. For the younger family member a computer becomes a valuable homework, revision and research tool.

Teleworking has given people the opportunity to work at home via a computer linked to their office. There is flexibility of working time, less need to physically commute between home and work, no need to provide office space, lighting and heating. An employer can recruit from a much wider geographical area.

For others teleworking can prove to be an unpleasant experience. There is the feeling of always being at work, being unable to cope with the distractions of the home environment, and a feeling of isolation.

The use of computer technology has changed dramatically the way in which businesses and industry operate. The term 'office automation' is used to express the manner in which most types of office functions are now performed using computers.

There are many other applications that are specially designed to help with the running and decision-making processes in business. These include Accounting Packages, Statistics Packages, Management Information Systems, and Decision Support Systems.

Computer aided design (CAD) and computer aided manufacturing (CAM) are two terms often linked with the use of computers in industry. CAD is a general term referring to software packages that are used to design an artefact. CAM is the use of computers and other automated equipment to control the production of an artefact. CAD/CAM refers to the linking of the software design tool to the automatic production.

Government agencies use computers to store and interrogate vast numbers of personal records.

Computers are used widely in many schools, colleges and training institutions. They are used not only for common administration, recording and production purposes, but also play a role in the process of education itself.

Computer Aided Learning, CAL, has many advantages. The learning material can be enriched providing a more stimulating environment. A student can work at his/her own pace, taking a different route through the material according to his/her ability, an exercise can be repeated as many times as the user wishes, and instant feedback can be gained from computer marked tests.

Disadvantages of CAL are that it can be laborious reading large amounts of information from a screen and valuable interaction between teacher and student is lost. A student cannot ask for something to be explained in a different manner, a lesson cannot be changed to suit a certain group of individuals, and some students need the discipline and motivational skills of a human teacher.

Computers never get tired, frustrated, hungry or angry, they can produce an extensive range of documents, and they can cross-reference facts derived from many different sources.

Computers have many disadvantages. They breakdown, training and recruiting people can be difficult and expensive, information systems need to be set-up and maintained by highly trained staff, and some people are fearful of computers which causes undue stress.

Computers can consistently carry out tasks at high speed with accuracy. A computer system can hold vast amounts of information in a very small space. Computers can carry out dangerous tasks or enter dangerous situations. They can provide a round-the-clock service

A human is better than a computer when the tasks to be performed are different each time. Humans are better when creativity is required, where judgement and experience are needed and where human feelings need to be taken into account.

Exercises.

1. State two disadvantages of working from home (teleworking).

2. Discuss two aspects of computers that make them a good choice for completing some tasks. Include appropriate tasks in your answer.

3. Explain the term MIS. Give an example of information that a MIS might provide for the manager of a leisure centre.

4. The introduction of a computer system at a supermarket will obviously bring about some changes. What might these changes be from the point of view of, a) the retailer, and b) the customer?

I.T. and Society

In this chapter you will learn how to

- *Understand the terms Information Society and Information Superhighway.*

- *Know implications of Year 2000 issue.*

- *Understand the concept of Electronic Commerce.*

- *Understand what elements and practices contribute to a good working environment.*

- *Be aware of Health and Safety precautions when using a computer.*

7.1. A Changing World

If we were able to transport ourselves into the future and look back we might label our time as the information age, just as we have labelled the stone, bronze, and iron ages. The industrial revolution saw a change in working practices where many people came in from working in the fields and the countryside to work in mills and factories.

Today many people are not employed in manufacturing jobs but in what is termed the service industry. Many of these people are information workers, using computers to capture, store, and process data. The results of this processing then needs to be prepared for communication in a suitable manner.

We are surrounded with access to a wealth of information of every kind, some might say smothered by it. This information can be accessed from within our homes and on the move in addition to our place of work. Indeed as advances are made our place of work is actually becoming harder to define. Accessing and using this information has become an essential skill of life today. We are said to be living in an 'Information Society'.

Information today is definitely a valuable commodity. Companies will pay a considerable sum for information they haven't got. This could be a list of names and addresses of people with a certain interest. This information becomes more valuable if it is sorted, for example, in terms of annual income, types of employment, or simply age. A company may use this information to mail people with advertising literature, selecting people who are most likely to be interested.

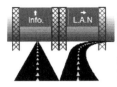 A main source of information for many is the Internet. Advancements made have improved the speed of access that enables huge amounts of information to quickly be communicated between source and destination. These advancements have led to the Internet being labelled the 'Information Superhighway'.

The Internet has in no doubt provided another significant dimension to the way in which computers have affected the way we live. The concept of electronic commerce, commonly termed simply 'e-commerce', is a new and significant change in the way we buy goods and services. E-commerce is a generic term used for the buying and selling of goods and services over the Internet.

There have been warnings to companies that to survive they must establish a presence on the Internet and embrace the concept of e-commerce. The possibility of global trade and the potential to reach millions of customers seems like too good an opportunity to miss. For some companies this has been a highly successful approach. Amazon.com has emerged as the world's largest bookshop in terms of books available. Some companies have not been successful. E-commerce does not only depend upon having an effective web site, but being able to provide the support for the custom gained this way. If a company does not want to restrict its trade and sell to a global market, can they cope with global deliveries and global finance?

In the United Kingdom common items purchased from Web sites are books, travel tickets and computer related products. However, many people are still afraid to shop this way due to the fear of credit card fraud. As long as a secure connection is used from a secure site, shopping this way can be much safer than giving out credit card details over the phone, or, letting a waiter in a restaurant disappear with the card for a period of time.

information

Examples of Web sites selling the products and services described above can be found at the following Web addresses:

The Internet Bookshop: http://www.bookshop.co.uk
The Train Line: http://www.thetrainline.co.uk
Time Computers: http://www.timecomputers.com

The dependence of today's society on computers was highlighted by the perceived threat of the millennium bug. The realisation that many computer systems might fail caused many hearts to falter and extreme cries of doom and gloom. In the event, depending on how you look at it, it was either a non-event, or most people prepared for it so well the predicted difficulties were sorted out beforehand.

The millennium bug was simply the fact that some computer systems only used two digits to store the date. 1980 was simply stored as 80, 1999 as 99, and so on. This was done to save memory and storage space on the early computer systems, not a problem on today's machines. Either the year 2000 seemed a long way off or it was plainly just not thought about.

Having a date of 00 instead of 2000 held different problems for different systems. It was just not accepted by many applications that declared the fact that you could not have a null date. 00 was mistakenly seen as 1900 having disastrous consequences for automated delivery dates scheduled after 1999. Even more disastrous was the prediction that some computers would simply just not start. Computers have an internal real-time clock that is checked on start-up. It is used, for example to date-stamp files. This wasn't as dire as first feared as many just defaulted to 1980 and carried on.

A global campaign made many aware of the difficulties and people with responsibility for I.T. systems coped with it. The interesting point to emerge was the near hysteria caused by the thought of not being able to access and process information. For many it cemented our reliance on the computer and its ability to process data.

7.2. A Good Workspace

For people who spend a long time at a computer either by choice or as a necessary part of their work, a good workspace is essential to one's well being. In the United Kingdom the Health and Safety Executive have published guidelines for the use of 'display screen equipment'. These regulations can help a computer user create a good workspace and adopt good working practices.

The computer screen is an important, yet often neglected, aspect of a computer system regarding its comfortable use. It is the item people spend most time looking at. It should be of adequate size displaying a stable image in a suitable resolution. In order to make viewing easy on the eyes a screen needs to be adjustable for brightness and contrast. When a screen has been switched on for a period of time it will warm up a little and the screen will increase in brightness. Users should remember to make appropriate adjustments after a period of use. The ability of the screen to swivel and tilt does not only make it easier to view but can help to eliminate glare. It may be necessary to install a window covering, or to reposition a computer in order to avoid screen glare. Try to sit with the top of the screen at eye level approximately 60cm from your eyes.

The keyboard is the most common method of inputting data into a computer system. Data input is much easier and more pleasant if a keyboard is able to tilt and there is space in front of the keyboard for the users hands and arms. A matt keyboard with clearly defined letters is a must. The keyboard should sit comfortably at your fingertips with your arms and hands sloping down slightly. Holding your wrists at a sharp angle can cause discomfort with prolonged use. Money spent on a good quality keyboard is a sound investment.

Having spent a good deal of money on a computer system many people give little thought to where they are going to use it and onto what they are going to place it. The work surface itself should be stable and have a matt finish. There ought to be adequate space for all the equipment and any documents that one might work from.

Being able to adopt a comfortable position at the workspace on a comfortable chair is important. The chair should have a five-point base to protect from overbalancing and be adjustable in height and tilt. A conscious effort should be made to sit so that your back is adequately supported. Your feet should be firmly on the ground or on a suitable footrest.

Adequate room lighting should be provided both to view the screen and other documents. This should be moderate and indirect, providing a low contrast between the screen and other lighting. Any lighting should take into account the possible glare caused.

Computer systems, like most large electrical devices, emit a degree of heat. Where there are perhaps several within one room, adequate ventilation and control of humidity levels may be necessary. Many large companies and institutions provide air-conditioned rooms in situations where many computer systems are used in close proximity to each other.

Users can help themselves in planning their work schedules. If possible take frequent breaks from the screen about every 1.5 hours. An employee could perhaps punctuate computer work with filing or telephone work. If such breaks are not possible then move your eyes frequently away from the screen, focusing them at a different distance.

7.3. Health and Safety

It is difficult for many to appreciate how a poorly designed workspace and bad working practice can cause serious health and safety problems. Opinions do differ on the extent of the problems that can occur from long term use of computers. There is no real consensus of opinion between professional bodies on such problems as repetitive strain injury, RSI, or the reported detrimental effects upon pregnant women of electromagnetic radiation emitted from a computer monitor.

However, some common potential dangers apply to the use of any electrical device. Computer equipment ought to be connected to the power supply with suitable cables that are in good condition, not frayed or worn. A full computer system generates the need for many electrical outlets. The computer base unit, monitor, printer, scanner and modem can all need access to an electrical socket. There is an obvious temptation to overload a socket using multiple adapters. Overloading instead of supplying suitable outlets leaves users liable to electrical shock and generates a real risk of fire within the property.

Computer cables connecting different hardware devices ought to follow a proper course. Leaving trailing cables near to where people work and across walkways is dangerous practice. There is an obvious risk of injury through tripping. A cable trailing off the end of a desk could catch a passing person potentially causing injury, but also there could be damage to the equipment.

As in other occupations, computer work can be monotonous. A data entry clerk will perform many repeated movements throughout a typical working day. Repetitive strain injury, RSI, is a term applied to problems that arise from such work. It usually manifests itself as numbness, stiffness, or tingling in the neck, shoulders, arms, hands, and fingers. A user suffering from RSI finds it difficult to pick up or lift items. This can be avoided by taking frequent breaks.

 Aching shoulders and arms, as well as an aching back, may not be caused by RSI but can be caused by bad posture. It is essential that a person who is going to be sat for long periods of time at a computer system adopts a correct posture. Avoid slouching or bending, whilst having one's back supported will help avoid problems.

Eyestrain is a common complaint that is levelled against the use of computers. Again there is no evidence to suggest this is true. A properly adjusted monitor with a screen that is free from glare should not affect a person's eyesight. A flickering screen, as with a flickering television, can cause nausea and affect people with epilepsy.

As well as physical difficulties it is worth considering the stress that the use of computers can cause. Change of any kind causes stress in people. Changing to a computer-based environment can cause great stress in some workers who do not feel competent or comfortable using computer systems. More senior colleagues can feel threatened by a more computer literate, possibly younger, person. In a less direct way, computers are often used to monitor the productivity of workers. The ability of computers to process data at high speed and present vast quantities of information can lead to a feeling of information overload. There are many, many working days lost each year through stress.

Summary

Today we are said to be living in an 'Information Society'. Many people are information workers, using computers to capture, store, and process data. We are provided with access to a wealth of information of every kind. This information can be accessed from within our homes, on the move, and from our place of work. Indeed as advances are made, our place of work is actually becoming hard to define.

Information today is a valuable commodity. Advancements made in improving the speed of access have led to the Internet being labelled the 'Information Superhighway'. E-commerce is a generic term used for the buying and selling of goods and services over the Internet. Common items purchased from Web sites are books, travel tickets and computer related products. Many people are still afraid to shop this way due to the fear of credit card fraud.

The millennium bug was simply the fact that some computer systems used two digits to store the date. 1980 was simply stored as 80, 1999 as 99, and so on. Having a date of 00 instead of 2000 gave rise to many potential problems.

For people who spend a long time at a computer, a good workspace is essential to one's well being. A computer user can create a good workspace and adopt good working practices by considering the computer screen viewed, the keyboard used, the work surface the system is placed upon, being able to adopt a comfortable seating position, and working in suitable lighting. Planning a work schedule involving frequent breaks can help avoid problems.

A poorly designed workspace and bad working practice can cause serious health and safety problems. Computer equipment ought to be connected to the power supply with suitable cables that are in good condition, not frayed or worn. Overloading of electrical sockets can leave users liable to electrical shock and create a risk of fire. Computer cables connecting different hardware devices ought to follow a proper course and be properly secured.

Repetitive strain injury, RSI, is a term applied to problems that arise from monotonous work involving repeated movements. It usually manifests itself as numbness, stiffness, or tingling in the neck, shoulders, arms, hands, and fingers. Aching shoulders and arms, as well as an aching back can be caused by bad posture. A properly adjusted monitor with a screen that is free from glare should not cause eyestrain

The use of computers can cause stress. Some workers do not feel competent or comfortable using computer systems. A computer can be used to monitor and track the productivity of workers. The ability of computers to process data at high speed and present vast quantities of information can lead to a feeling of information overload.

Exercises

1. Briefly explain the term 'e-commerce' and highlight a fear that a person may have concerning its use.

2. Describe three aspects of a badly designed workspace that can have a detrimental effect on a person's health or safety.

3. Briefly describe three common injuries that are often attributed to a badly designed workspace.

4. Using an example highlight a difficulty that could arise due to the millennium bug.

5. What is the 'Information Superhighway' and what role might it play in justifying the claim that we are living in an 'Information Society'.

Security, Copyright and the Law

In this chapter you will learn how to

- *Know the purpose and value of backing-up computer files.*

- *Know how to protect a personal computer against intrusion.*

- *Understand the privacy issues associated with personal computers.*

- *Know what happens to data and files in the event of a power cut.*

- *Understand what a computer virus is and how it can enter a system.*

- *Know about anti-virus measures.*

- *Understand the security and legal issues related to software.*

- *Understand the terms freeware, shareware, and user licences.*

- *Understand the implications of the Data Protection Act.*

- *Be able to describe some of the uses of personal data.*

8.1. Security

Computer data files can be the lifeblood of a company. They can also hold important data for an individual, perhaps an essential project, vital account information, or perhaps examination coursework. It makes sense to take copies of these files in case the original files become corrupt. Files can become corrupt for many reasons such as operating system failure, power being removed from the computer before it has been closed properly, virus infection, and perhaps malicious damage.

The location of the backup copies is important. There is little use in keeping backups in close proximity to the originals as whatever catastrophe befalls the originals may effect the backups. Copies of important files should be saved regularly onto portable storage media and clearly labelled. If the originals are then lost or damaged, they can be recovered from the backup storage.

Files of a small size can be backed up to 3.5" floppy disk that will hold 1.44Mb of data. Some larger files can also be stored to 3.5" floppy disk but they firstly need to be compressed using special software so that they take up less space than the originals.

The larger files, or a large number of files, typically need special consideration. It would be difficult and not very practical to backup a hard disk drive onto many floppy disks. A more practical solution would be to use another hard disk or a tape backup system. Restoring the files of a whole hard drive from tape can take quite a while.

It is a wise policy to keep backup copies of files in a different physical location than the originals. For really valuable data they should preferably be stored in a safe fireproof location to guard against the premises containing the files being destroyed by a fire or other natural disaster.

Valuable data can be lost if a computer system is subjected to intrusion from unauthorised personnel. Measures to stop unauthorised access should also be taken to protect sensitive or confidential information. In fact, in some instances people have a legal obligation to take measures to protect data.

There are several measures that can be taken. These may include physically locking the computer within a cabinet or room allowing only certain people to have keys. Entry to a room can again be restricted by the use of swipe cards. For many a more practical solution is the use of passwords.

A computer system can have passwords set that allow access at various levels. Access to a certain drive, a directory, or a single file can be restricted by the user having to type a suitable password. An administrator may have full access to all drives and applications along with the ability to set, edit and remove other people's level of access. At the other end of the spectrum, a guest type password may only allow access to one application and the use of a removable drive. More than one level of access can be set on a single computer. Different people logging on to a system with the same level of password may see a different, personalised desktop, but the same restrictions on drives and directories will still apply.

definition

Logging on: The act of having to type in a password to gain access to a system. A password when entered usually appears as a series of stars, *.

Desktop: The way that the graphical user interface presents itself to the user. It usually consists of icons on a background giving shortcuts to applications that the user frequently uses.

In order for a password system to be effective the users need to adopt an effective policy. Users should remember the purpose is security and that passwords should never be revealed. The passwords of at least five characters need to be remembered and not written down. They ought to be changed on a regular basis. This change can be enforced by the computer system itself with previous recent passwords not being allowed. When changing a password the user will usually have to enter it twice in order to verify correct entry.

Common bad practice is simply adding a number to the end of a password and incrementing this number when requested to change it. This is ineffective if the original password has been compromised. Choosing the name of a child, a favourite team, favourite player, or even location, whose name appears below a photograph on the person's desk, is again not good idea. The often-used mothers' maiden name can be compromised if people know a little of your history.

Preventing unauthorised access to networks is a problem, particularly if they are linked to the Internet. Many install what is known as a 'firewall'. This is specialist software that scrutinises all information entering and leaving a network. Information that does not meet the criteria specified is rejected. Another precaution to prevent networks being invaded from outside is the use of a call back system. When a system is accessed from a remote location outside of the network, possibly via a modem, the system hangs up and calls the user back on a predetermined number allocated only to an authorised user.

Encryption can be used to protect data files that are incoming or outgoing from the network, such as confidential E-mail. Encryption uses specialist software to scramble data before transmission. The receiving person can only read the message if they have the same specialist software.

Data can be lost if power is removed from a system. When working on a computer your work is stored in RAM. Unfortunately RAM is volatile, anything stored there is lost once power is removed. Remove power from RAM and it forgets everything. The result is that anything that has been stored in RAM since you last saved a file will be lost. It is good practice to get into the habit of saving your work on a regular basis. Some of the more recent word processing packages can be configured to automatically save work at set time periods.

Most networks employ a device known as an uninterruptible power supply, UPS, that will maintain power to a network long enough for essential data to be saved in the event of power loss.

Obtaining illegal access to data has been given its own term, 'hacking'. It is now a well-publicised form of computer crime. Hacking is not as great a problem these days as security and detection have become much more sophisticated. Grown out of this crime is phone fraud, known as 'phreaking'.

One of the greatest problems for the hacker was the amount of time they needed to be on-line and thus the tremendous phone bills that this generates. A similar problem exists with the amount of time spent on the Internet. One of the first tasks a hacker might do was to defer his/her phone costs on to someone else. Some large companies have paid substantial phone bills for computer criminals. At one time the voice-mail messages of large companies were an easy target. This crime often came to the notice of the company when large phone bills were charged for weekends when they were closed! Today, security and detection is much more sophisticated.

8.2. Computer Viruses

A computer virus is a piece of computer code that was written to cause damage, recover data illegally, or simply cause annoyance. Virus is an apt term as the main goal of such code is to survive, reproduce and damage a computer system just like a biological virus in a living body. Computer viruses are no respecters of boundaries or status and can travel at lightening speed. In the year 2000 the 'I Love You' virus utilised the Internet to travel: originating in the Philippines, it had spread globally within hours. It also highlighted the vulnerability of computer systems despite sophisticated protection measures. A virus originating from a small personal computer within hours had closed down networks within government agencies and multinational companies.

Viruses usually attach themselves to executable files enabling them to spread each time the file is opened. Some of those that travel via the Internet use a person's personal e-mail address book to reproduce and spread. Those that attach to other types of file may corrupt the data within the file but won't actually reproduce. Viruses spread either via contaminated removable disks being passed between computers, or they are innocently downloaded via a network or Internet connection.

Sometimes users are unaware that their system has been infected. Symptoms that may indicate infection are, the computer may run very slowly, files may disappear, files are reported as being corrupt, areas of memory become inaccessible, or applications simply won't run because they no longer fit into RAM. Some types of virus are not so subtle and will inform the user by displaying some kind of message on the screen.

One of the worst types of virus can attack the file allocation table, (FAT), on your hard disk. The FAT is used by the operating system in order to locate files. It is a map providing directions to all your data. Without it, the hard disk is unusable. Such an attack usually results in having to format the infected hard drive creating a new FAT and enabling the disk to be used again. Unfortunately, formatting will also destroy all the data formerly stored on the hard disk.

A good virus software package is an excellent guard against infection. It is important to use the latest version and make sure that it is kept up to date. Anti-virus software is only effective against strains of virus that it is aware of. A good package from a reputable source will offer free updates for registered users in order to deal with new viruses. These can often be downloaded from the Internet. Virus protection software can be set to constantly scan your system for any changes. It can then warn the user if a virus is present before it has chance to do any damage. The anti-virus software itself should be able to clean disks and rid a system of infection.

If a system is clean from the start the only way that infection can occur is from outside. Accepting this fact a user can take some simple precautions to help protect themselves. A user ought to virus check any unfamiliar disks before using them in addition to checking one's own disks that have been used outside one's own system.

Since viruses spread by attaching themselves onto existing files, so simply write protecting a disk can stop infection. If a disk is write protected then it can only be read from and not written to. Commercially produced software is unlikely to be infected, and even less likely if it is distributed on CD-ROM. Some people still scan such software in an effort to be safe rather than sorry.

8.3. Copyright

When buying commercial software what you are actually purchasing is a copy of the software and the right to use it, you are not buying ownership of the software. You simply licence the right to use it. All commercial software contains a software licence agreement that sets out the terms and conditions under which you are entitled to use it. Read all license agreements carefully and make sure that your use of software is in compliance with the license issued with it, otherwise you could be breaking the law.

Each piece of software sold has a unique serial number. There is usually a registration card inside the package. Either fill in this card and send it back to the address in the documentation, or alternatively, you can usually register 'on-line' via the Internet. When you register your software, the distributor has a record that you have purchased their product.

Being a registered user has its advantages. You could be eligible for upgrades to later versions of the product for free or at considerably less cost than purchasing the new version. Many software producers also send relevant information to their registered users with details of the software purchased or other products that may be of interest. Even though you may have taken great care of the original program disks, accidents do happen. If at a later date these originals are damaged, the distributor may be prepared to help registered users.

By installing the program you are agreeing to the licence terms. The purchaser is usually allowed to make one copy of legally purchased software as a personal backup. Copying for any other purpose is software piracy, which is illegal. It is also illegal to knowingly use pirated software even though you may not have copied it.

The most common licence is a single user licence for use by one person at a time on one machine. Some single user licence agreements will allow the purchaser to install the software onto a portable computer as well as a desktop as long as both are not used at the same time. This allows for the fact that a user may be out and about during the day working with an application on a laptop, but may wish to download data to a desktop once back at the office.

When there are many users within a company who wish to use the software at the same time, then either multiple copies of the software can be purchased, or a site licence or a multi-user licence agreement can be bought if one is available. These multi-user and site licences are usually offered at a much reduced cost compared to single licences. However, they may not come complete with any documentation, or maybe one set, including user manuals. Additional manuals are usually available to be purchased separately.

Sharing files across a network is deemed to be multiple use. A licence must be purchased to cover the maximum possible numbers of users of the software at any one time.

As well as this strictly commercial software, public domain software is available. This is usually distributed on disk or can be downloaded from the Internet. This public domain software is often referred to as either Shareware or Freeware. The authors of shareware allow you to try their program for free, and if you like it and want to continue to use it, ask you to pay a fee. Some shareware programs are time limited and will cease to function after a short period of time following installation, for example after a month.

Freeware can be freely copied and used. It is quite rare and always contains a notice within the program stating that use of the software is free of charge. Large commercial companies will sometimes distribute cut-down freeware versions of applications they wish to sell. These cut-down versions will not have full functionality available, for example the ability to save files has often been disabled.

8.4. Data Protection Act

Computers are very efficient tools at gathering and sorting data. For this reason it was felt that there needed to be some legislation to protect the rights of the individual whenever personal data was stored or processed automatically. Many countries now have in statute a Data Protection Act – a misleading title as it is really about protecting the individual not the actual data. Employers and employees are legally obliged to protect other people's privacy. Compliance with the Council of European Convention on Data Protection enables data to flow between European countries.

Interpretation of the Data Protection Act can be a little confusing. At present it only applies to data that is processed automatically, although in the future full compliance will extend to paper based documents that are processed manually. Information relating to living identifiable individuals is covered, not information relating to a company or organisation. Personal data covers statements of fact and expressions of opinion about an individual. Confusion can arise when the exemptions are considered.

There are some quite straightforward reasonable exemptions. Exemption is made over:

● Data that is needed to safeguard national security or enforcement of the law.
● Data held for the payment of wages and pensions.
● Data held for the recording of purchases and sales.
● Personal data held by an individual for personal, family, household affairs and for recreational purposes.

Care must be taken over exemptions such as:

- Personal data held for distributing articles or information to people. This exemption is small and only really relates to names and addresses.
- Personal data held by members of a club. Each person must be a member of the club and be asked if they mind the data being held for this purpose.
- Word processed data. The act does not cover information entered onto a computer for the sole purpose of editing text and printing out the document.

The Data Protection Act stipulates that users of personal data must register certain facts with a Data Registrar. Personal data must be:

- Obtained and processed lawfully and fairly.
- Only used for the purpose stated when registering the intentions with the Data Registrar.
- Only disclosed to those people described in the register entry.
- Adequate, relevant and not excessive.
- Accurate and kept up-to-date.
- Held no longer than is necessary.
- Accessible to the individual concerned who has the right to have the information corrected or erased.
- Held securely.

Personal data is put to a wide spectrum of uses. Some examples of situations where privacy should be respected concern medical reports, details of credit ratings, and employee assessments. In each of these instances an individual would, in addition to privacy, expect that the information is accurate, relevant and kept up-to-date.

If the Act is breached by accident or by deliberate misuse, then the person in control of the data could have to pay considerable financial penalties. For some companies this may pale in comparison to a loss of public confidence.

Summary

Backup copies of essential files should be taken and kept in a secure location. These are taken in case the original files become corrupt. Files can become corrupt for many reasons such as operating system failure, power being removed from the computer before it has been closed properly, virus infection, and perhaps malicious damage. A fire or other natural disaster can also destroy original files.

Measures to stop unauthorised access should also be taken to protect sensitive or confidential information. These may include physically locking the computer within a cabinet or room, restricting entry by the use of swipe cards, or the use of a password system. In order for a password system to be effective the users need to adopt an effective policy. Passwords should be of at least five characters, not revealed to anyone, not written down, and ought to be changed on a regular basis.

To prevent networks being invaded from outside the use of a firewall or a call back system can be employed. Encryption can also be used to protect data files that are incoming or outgoing from the network.

Data can be lost if power is removed from a system. RAM is volatile, anything stored there is lost once power is removed. Save work on a regular basis.

Hacking is obtaining illegal access to data.

A computer virus is simply a piece of computer code that was written to cause damage, recover data illegally, or cause annoyance. Viruses usually attach themselves to executable files enabling them to spread each time the file is opened. Some of those that travel via the Internet use a person's personal e-mail address book to reproduce and spread. Those that attach to other types of file may corrupt the data within the file but won't actually reproduce.

A good anti-virus software package is a good guard against infection. It is important to use the latest version and make sure that it is kept up to date as anti-virus software is only effective against strains of virus that it is aware of. A user ought to virus check any unfamiliar disks before using them in addition to checking their own disks that have been used outside their own system. Write protecting a disk can stop infection.

All commercial software contains a software licence agreement that sets out the terms and conditions under which you are entitled to use it. By installing the program you are agreeing to the licence terms. The purchaser is usually allowed to make one copy of legally purchased software as a personal backup

Each piece of software sold has a unique serial number. When you register your software, the distributor has a record that you have purchased their product. Possible advantages of registration are being eligible for upgrades, receiving further relevant information, and possible help if original disks are damaged.

A single user licence is for use by one person at a time on one machine. When there are many users within a company a site licence, or a multi-user licence can be bought if one is available.

Shareware allows you to try a program for free, and if you want to continue to use it, you must pay a fee. Freeware can be freely copied and used.

The Data Protection Act is legislation designed to protect the rights of the individual whenever personal data is stored or processed automatically.

There are some exemptions, but essentially the Act states that personal data must be:

- Obtained and processed lawfully and fairly.
- Only used for the stated purpose.
- Only disclosed to those people described in the register entry.
- Adequate relevant and not excessive.
- Accurate and kept up-to-date.
- Held no longer than is necessary.
- Accessible to the individual concerned who has the right to have the information corrected or erased.
- Held securely.

Exercises

1. State two ways in which you can protect data stored as computer files from unauthorised access.

2. State three ways in which you can reduce the risk of infections from a computer virus.

3. What is the difference between freeware and shareware?

4. Generally what rights to copy software does a single user licence grant to a user.

5. Give two examples of personal data usage that are exempt from the Data Protection Act.

Answer Guide

The following section contains sample and suggested answers to all of the exercises in this guide.

1. Getting Started

1.1 Briefly describe, using examples, the difference between hardware and software.

The term hardware relates to the physical aspects of a computer system whilst software refers to the programs that run on a computer to perform certain tasks. Examples of hardware include printer, monitor, keyboard, mouse and speaker. Examples of software are Windows 98, word processing, spreadsheet and database packages. Any other relevant software packages.

1.2 Name three different types of computer systems and comment on possible suitable uses for them.

Any three with appropriate use from:

● Supercomputer. For weather forecasting.
● Mainframe. Large scale data processing needs, for example within banks and insurance companies.
● Mini computer. Storing a large shared database.
● Personal Computer. Calculating expense account details.
● Portable Computer. Taking notes at a business meeting.

1.3 Name three peripheral devices. State whether they are input or output devices.

Any three suitable devices with correct specification. Examples include:

● Keyboard   Input
● Mouse   Input
● Monitor   Output
● Printer   Output
● Speaker   Output
● Barcode reader Input
● Plotter   Output
● Light pen   Input

1.4 From where does the term "PC" derive?

The term PC derives from the name 'Personal Computer'. The first type of computer developed that was small enough to fit on a desktop.

1.5 Describe the difference between a dumb terminal and an intelligent terminal.

A dumb terminal does not have its own processing power, being reliant upon a central network server. It is common for such a terminal to be without any storage capability.

An intelligent terminal is capable of processing data and has its own storage devices, being able to function to a certain degree independently of a central server.

1.6 Describe two advantages of using a network.
Any two from:

- Sharing of work files.
- Sharing of hardware devices.
- Being able to communicate with other network users.
- Security.

2. Hardware

2.1 What basic functions does a microprocessor perform? How is its clock speed measured?
A microprocessor is responsible for executing the software, communication with external devices, and reading and writing to memory.

The speed of a microprocessor is measured in Hertz, Hz. One Hz is one clock cycle per second.

2.2 When using a mouse the shape of the cursor may change to reflect its use. Name two specific shapes of cursor and state a particular instance where it may be seen.
Any two from:

Pointer	To select menu items, files, or graphics.
I – Beam	To place the cursor within a text document.
Crosshairs	To draw lines, circles etc within a graphics package.

2.3 Name and briefly describe the use of three output devices other than a monitor and a printer.
Any three from:

● Speaker	To hear sounds generated by the system.
● Microfilm	To view archived documents.
● Plotter	To produce hardcopy output of drawn elements and basic text in a format greater than A4.
● Speech synthesisers	To generate standard messages delivered to the user.

2.4 State two factors that affect the quality of display on a computer monitor.

● The size of the screen, which is measured diagonally.
● The resolution of the screen. The number of pixels displayed per inch/cm and the number of lines scanned that make up the screen.

3. Storage

3.1 Explain the terms bit and byte. How are these terms related to a character and a field?

A bit is a single binary digit, a 1 or a 0. A byte consists of 8 bits.
Each character is represented by a byte of data. A field consists of a number of characters, and therefore a number of bytes.

3.2 Explain how main memory (RAM) and secondary storage are used for the storage of programs.

Program instructions and data are loaded into main memory from where they are accessed whilst the program runs. Programs are saved for long-term use onto secondary storage media, such as a disk. Main memory is erased when power is removed.

3.3 A well-meaning friend advises you on how to improve your computer performance. They suggest:

a) Installing more RAM.
b) Installing a faster processor.
c) Changing the type of mouse used.
d) Reducing the number of programs running at any one time.

Which courses of action do you think might help and which would not?

a), b) and d) all help to improve performance. Whilst changing the mouse may provide an improved interface for the user, it does not improve performance.

3.4 Briefly describe three different secondary storage devices stating a typical application, an advantage and a disadvantage.

Any three from:

Device	Application	Advantage	Disadvantage
3.5" Floppy disk	Storing work files	Highly Portable	Small capacity, slow access

Hard disk	Storing of work and programs	Large capacity, fast access	Generally not portable
CD-ROM	Distribution of software	Quite large capacity, portable	Read only
Tape drive	Archiving of data	Large capacity	Slow access

4. Software

4.1 Explain the difference between systems software and applications software stating an example of each.

System software helps to run the computer. It helps to control all of the hardware and ensure that it all works together. Examples include versions of Windows, MSDOS, Linux, and OS2.

Application software is software designed to perform a specific task. Examples include word processing, spreadsheets, or DTP.

4.2 Name an advantage of both a GUI and a command line interface.

Advantages of a GUI are that there are no commands to learn in order to achieve something, all programs run in the same manner, and all the programs have the same look and feel about them.

Advantages of a command line interface are that for an experienced user it can be an efficient way to work, and it is less demanding in terms of computer hardware.

4.3 Give three functions of an operating system.

Any three from:

a. Managing the allocation of memory.
b. Loading and unloading of programs.
c. Execution of programs.
d. Saving of work.
e. Controlling input and output devices.
f. 'Booting up' the computer.
g. Checking and controlling user access.
h. Logging of errors.

4.4 Briefly describe three application packages and state a typical use.

Any three suitable packages and description, including:

- A word processing package which will allow a user to type, correct, delete and move text. The font size, alignment and style can be changed. The ability to check spelling and grammar are included in most packages. Word processing packages are used to produce documents such as letters, reports, books and articles.
- Spreadsheet packages are used to store and manipulate tables of numerical data. Complex formulae can be entered and copied. Predefined mathematical functions can be used and several different types of graphs set-up. Uses of spreadsheets include financial accounting, statistical analysis, and financial modelling
- Database packages are used for the storage and retrieval of information. These packages allow users to set up tables of data and to link them together. These sets of linked data can then be searched according to certain criteria stipulated by the user. Databases are extensively used for storing library book stock detail and loan management, customer details, and order and delivery details.
- Desktop publishing allows the user to layout a page exactly as he or she wants it. They allow the entry of text, diagrams, and photographs in a variety of formats. Text from one box can be made to flow into another. DTP packages are used extensively for the production of such items as advertising leaflets, booklets and newsletters.
- Graphics packages are used to produce artwork. Images can be imported from and stored in a variety of formats, reflected, rotated and reduced or expanded in size. These packages are used by a wide variety of people including artists, animators, architects, and engineers.
- Presentation packages are used for presenting information to an audience. They allow for the inputting of text, numerical data, graphs, and images. The presentation can be constructed on a number of slides. These can be used for promoting the sale of a product, selling an idea, or presenting an action plan.

4.5 List three tasks you can accomplish easily on a word processor that you could not easily do on a typewriter.

Three suitable tasks including:

- Use pre-prepared templates.
- Store text and recall it later for editing.
- Easily change fonts and styles.
- Automatically spell check documents.
- Cut, copy and paste text to different locations.

4.6 State three advantages of presenting learning using multimedia and one possible disadvantage.

The advantages of multimedia include:

- Multimedia is more varied and flexible than a book.
- It is interactive.
- Specific feedback on certain actions can be given.
- Huge volumes of information can be searched in a non-laborious fashion.
- The user can usually take a variety of paths through the material.

Disadvantages are:

- There is a need for special equipment.
- Reading large amounts from a screen can be tiring.
- Portability is a problem.

4.7 During the development of a software package state the purpose of beta testing.

Beta testing is the release of software to selected users for the purpose of testing. This gives the developers the opportunity to test the software on different types of hardware.

5. Information Networks

5.1 What is the difference between a LAN and a WAN?

A Local Area Network, (LAN) is one in which the connected computers are relatively close together, within a single room, floor, or building.

A Wide Area Network, (WAN) is one that covers a wider geographical area, connecting computers that are often quite remote. A WAN will often use the telephone network to communicate between users in these remote locations.

5.2 State an advantage and a disadvantage of using each of the telephone, Fax, and e-mail.

Answers could include:

Device	Advantage	Disadvantage
Telephone	Considered more personal. Can gauge the reaction by the tone of voice used.	No hard copy of conversation recorded. Direct one-to-one
Fax	Can send diagrams as well as text. Hard copy can be kept for reference.	Difficult to edit hard copy received. Copy of graphics is of a low quality.

| E-mail | Can easily send to more than one person at once. Local rate call to anywhere. Easy global communication. Original documents can be sent. | Expensive equipment needed. Junk e-mail can be received. |

5.3 Briefly describe the relationship between the Internet and the World Wide Web.

The Internet refers to the physical resources used to form a worldwide network of computers. The WWW is the actual software interface that allows us to search and view information held at specific 'web sites' on the Internet.

5.4 What facilities are needed to provide a user with access to the Internet?

● A computer.
● A telephone connection.
● A modem or ISDN card.
● Internet Service Provider software.

5.5 Describe the difference between analogue and digital signals.

● A digital signal is one that is seen to be physically in one state or its opposite, at one of two opposite extremes.
● Analogue signals can be at either extreme or at any value in-between.

5.6 What is a modem used for and how is its speed specified?

A modem is a device that allows a digital computer to be connected to an analogue telephone line. The digital computer data is converted, or modulated, into analogue signals that can be used over the telephone line, and vice versa.

Its speed is specified by its baud rate. This is the maximum number of bits per second it is capable of transmitting, b.p.s.

6. Computers in Everyday Life

6.1 State two disadvantages of working from home (teleworking).

Any two from:

- There is the feeling of always being at work.
- The distractions of the home.
- The feeling of pressure to perform in an effort to keep up with office based colleagues
- The feeling of isolation from colleagues.

6.2 Discuss two aspects of computers that make them a good choice for completing some tasks. Include appropriate tasks in your answer.
Any two including:

- Speed. The ability to sort an extensive list of payments by their due date within a fraction of a second.
- Consistency. When the same calculation needs to be repeated many times, for example when calculating a monthly wage.
- Storage Capability. The ability to store vast amounts of data coupled with the ability to search this data. Consider a database of registered car owners being searched to find the owner of an abandoned car.

6.3 Explain the term MIS. Give an example of information that a MIS might provide for the manager of a leisure centre.
MIS refers to Management Information System. The purpose of such a system is to provide the right information to different levels of management.

For a leisure centre manager it could provide, for example, a summary of all the bookings taken for a particular activity on a particular day of the week. This information can be used to identify popular activities and busy times of the week.

6.4 The introduction of a computer system at a supermarket will obviously bring about some changes. What might these changes be from the point of view of, a) the retailer, and b) the customer?
a. From the retailers point of view:
- Save time on manual work.
- Accurate pricing.
- Facilitates stock control.
- Facilitates ordering.

b. From the point of view of the customer:
- Speeds up service.
- More information on receipts.
- Reduced personal service.

7. I.T. and Society

7.1 Briefly explain the term 'e-commerce' and highlight a fear that a person may have concerning its use.

E-commerce, electronic commerce, is a generic term used for the buying and selling of goods and services over the Internet. Many people are still afraid to shop this way due to security fears related to credit card fraud, which is how most purchases are paid for.

7.2 Describe three aspects of a badly designed workspace that can have a detrimental effect on a person's health or safety.

Any three including:

● Connections to the power supply made with cables that are not suitable or are in a poor condition.
● Overloading electrical sockets.
● Leaving trailing cables.
● Not utilising a screen of suitable size and resolution that is adjustable for brightness and contrast.
● Not eliminating glare on the screen.
● Not adopting a comfortable seating position a suitable distance from the screen.
● Having a crowded workspace with no room in front of the keyboard for hands and arms.
● The work surface not being stable and not having a matt finish.
● Not having adequate room lighting.
● A badly organised work schedule without frequent breaks from the screen.

7.3 Briefly describe three common injuries that are often attributed to a badly designed workspace.

Any three including:

● Prolonged, repetitive movements can give rise to repetitive strain injury, RSI. The symptoms of this are numbness, stiffness, or tingling in the neck, shoulders, arms, hands, and fingers.
● Aching shoulders and arms, as well as an aching back can be caused by bad posture.
● Prolonged use can cause temporary eyestrain.
● Stress concerning a fear of working with computers.

7.4 Using an example highlight a difficulty that could arise due to the millennium bug.

Any suitable example, including:

● 00 not being accepted by an application as it sees it as an invalid date.
● 00 mistakenly being seen as 1900, 01 as 1901 etc. This may result in a system seeing all orders for the year 2000+ as already delivered.

● Some computers simply not starting. Some computers might fail on an invalid date when this is checked at start-up.

7.5 What is the 'Information Superhighway' and what role might it play in justifying the claim that we are living in an 'Information Society'?

Improved speed of access to the Internet, a main source of information enabling huge amounts of information to quickly be communicated, have led to the Internet being labelled the 'Information Superhighway'.

The realisation of the extent to which society is dependant on information and the fact that many people are 'information workers', has led to the belief that we are living in an 'Information Society'.

8. Security, Copyright and the Law

8.1 State two ways in which you can protect data stored as computer files from unauthorised access.

Any two suitable methods including:
● Physically restricting access.
● Use of passwords.
● Encryption of data.
● Use of a firewall.

8.2 State three ways in which you can reduce the risk of infections from a computer virus.

● Write protect disks.
● Install and use recognised anti-virus software.
● Check unfamiliar disks before use.

8.3 What is the difference between freeware and shareware?

● Freeware can be used and distributed without cost.
● Shareware can usually only be used on a trial basis for a limited time period after which payment should be made to the author.

8.4 Generally what rights to copy software does a single user licence grant to a user?

A single user licence allows a person to use the software on only one machine at any one time. Some single user licence agreements will allow a person to install the software onto a portable computer as well as a desktop as long as both are not used at the same time. Usually only a single copy for backup purposes can be taken.

8.5 Give two examples of personal data usage that are exempt from the Data Protection Act.

Any two from:

- Data that is needed to safeguard national security or enforcement of the law.
- Data held for the payment of wages and pensions.
- Data held for the recording of purchases and sales.
- Personal data held by an individual for personal, family, household affairs and for recreational purposes.
- Data held for distributing articles or information to people. This exemption is small and only really relates to names and addresses.
- Personal data held by members of a club where each person must be a member of the club and consent to the data being held for this purpose.
- Word processed data for the sole purpose of editing text and printing out the document.

Index

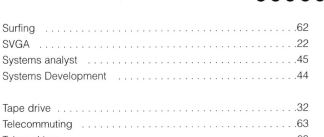

European Computer Driving Licence™

the european pc skills standard

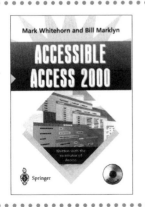